Cooking
with
Annemarie

OTHER BOOKS BY ANNEMARIE HUSTE

Annemarie's Personal Cookbook
How to Equip a Kitchen
Annemarie's Cookingschool Cookbook
Good Food

Cooking with Annemarie

A Revised Edition of *Good Food*

Annemarie Huste

A GD/PERIGEE BOOK

To
Edna Smith
and
Heidi Glocksien,
with many thanks for helping and making my life so much easier
and always being there to make me look good.
My daughter Bea,
who is the best.
And for
my beloved Dennis,
who has brought much joy into my life.

Perigee Books
are published by
The Putnam Publishing Group
200 Madison Avenue
New York, New York 10016

Illustrations by Linda Davrio

Library of Congress Cataloging in Publication Data

Huste, Annemarie.
Cooking with Annemarie.

Rev. ed. of: Good food, c1979.
"GD/Perigee book."
Includes index.
1. Cookery.   I. Huste, Annemarie. Good food. II. Title.
TX715.H9387   1984   641.5   83-21232
ISBN 0-399-51012-5

First Perigee printing, 1984
Printed in the United States of America
2 3 4 5 6 7 8 9

Contents

Introduction

I decided I wanted to write this book to tell you not only about some of my favorite recipes, but how you can select fresh, high-quality food, as well as how to treat it once you have found it. I also wanted to share knowledge about some of my favorite tools for the kitchen, which have made cooking more fun and easier than it has ever been. People talk about the good old days, but believe me, I know they weren't always good. I can recall making a salmon mousse before the age of food processors, and it took me hours in preparation and cleanup. Today, it takes about five minutes for the same chores. Availability of a variety of ingredients has improved too. For example, ten years ago a kiwi fruit wasn't even known in most places. Today it is almost a standard item in all produce sections in the country.

While traveling around the United States in the past years to do cooking classes to raise funds for various charities, such as museums and symphonies, I have met thousands of wonderful people. It is their generosity and hospitality that I would like to acknowledge in this book. They have shown me why America is the terrific country it is.

Equipment in the Kitchen

People always ask me what equipment they should buy for their kitchens. The answer can vary drastically depending on your lifestyle, the space you have available and your budget. There are some definite rules and some myths. The biggest myth on the subject is that a good cook can cook in anything. Well, that might hold true for an emergency but it certainly doesn't hold true on a day-to-day basis. Remember, a cook is not a magician; your dishes will be only as good as the ingredients and the tools you use allow.

Today there is such a variety of choices—whether it be pots or knives or food processors—that you should learn which one will work best for you before you buy it. In order to do this, you must be informed about the various products, and that is what I would like to do in this chapter.

Pots and Pans

Let's start with the most important kitchen items—pots and pans—and examine the materials they are made of and the pros and cons of each of them. Here's your first rule: the main purpose of having pots and pans is to cook in them, not to coordinate with the colors in your kitchen. A pan will serve that main purpose only if it conducts heat from the source, whether it be gas or electric, to the food. The more evenly the heat is conducted the better the food will cook. Each of the materials used to make pots and pans has a different conductivity, and thus, which one you choose may make a big difference in the final result.

Copper.

Copper has a long tradition in fine cooking because it is an excellent conductor of heat. This means that the heat spreads quickly and evenly over the pot's surface. A well-made heavy-gauge copper pan is a joy to cook in. With few exceptions (such as cooking sugar) copper must be lined with another metal because its direct contact with food can cause harmful chemical reactions. The best linings are tin and silver. Both these linings are fairly fragile and can be damaged by metal utensils and excessive heat. Pots lined with silver or tin must be relined periodically. Unfortunately, those that are lined with stainless steel are generally only thinly coated with copper and as a result are of very little use for cooking. The one thing they will certainly do for you is make you polish a lot of copper. Copper pans may be expensive, but if you're a very serious cook they may be worth the investment.

Aluminum.

Aluminum has come into great favor in recent years because it is a good heat conductor and is light and relatively inexpensive. This, of course, does not mean that every aluminum pot or pan is fit to cook in. To be really effective, the pan must be of heavy-gauge metal. If it is not, the heat will spread too fast and burn your food. One of the drawbacks to aluminum is that it will pit and tarnish when exposed to certain acids and alkalis. This will not result in any danger, as in the case of copper, but will affect the color of your food. Never cook with wine, lemon juice, or egg yolks in aluminum. It will turn your sauce into a disaster.

Cast Iron.

Cast-iron cookware, for all its faults, still retains some amount of popularity. Cast iron is a fairly even conductor of heat and retains high heat very effectively. This makes it an ideal metal in which to brown food. Because it is a very porous metal, the pans must be treated before use, meaning the thousands of tiny holes in the surface must be filled with oil. Some pans come preseasoned, but you will have to repeat the process from time to time because the oil eventually becomes rancid. Cast iron is very heavy, difficult to clean, and even damp weather will cause it to rust.

If there is a tradition of cast-iron cookware in your family, try to talk your mother out of hers. If you buy new pots and pans, you won't be happy with them until after a year of pain. If you must, however, the safest way to start the seasoning is to clean the pan well with soap and water, dry it thoroughly, then rub the pan well with vegetable oil. Put it into a 350°F. oven for about 30 minutes, then turn off heat and cool the pan in the oven.

Carbon Steel.

Carbon steel is popular with many chefs because, being sheet metal, it heats very quickly. This makes it ideal for restaurant fast frying. It is porous metal and will rust without proper care. Generally speaking, I find it too limited for home use. In addition, it is just as difficult to care for as cast iron.

Enamelware.

These pans generally conduct heat very well, and the enamel coating makes them impervious to acids. They are also easy to clean. However, the good ones are very heavy. I find them too heavy to lift even when they are empty. They have a tendency to chip, and if this happens to the cooking surface, you should not use them again. If they chip on the outside, they no longer look attractive, and let's face it, that's why most people buy them.

Silverstone, Teflon, T-Fal, etc.

Pans made with any of the above coatings work superbly for making omelettes and crêpes, and of course they are easy to clean. Their quality varies depending on what material is used and the thickness of the metal. All of them, regardless of their claims, eventually scratch and have to be replaced. You should consider that carefully before you buy them.

Pyrex, Corning Ware, etc.

The heat conduction of these pans is very poor. Once they absorb heat they retain it for a long time. They are strictly for oven and baking use. I use a Pyrex double boiler, however, solely because I can watch and control the boiling water.

Stainless Steel.

One of the most popular materials in use today is stainless steel. The quality varies according to the amount of nickel and chromium in it. The higher the ratio of nickel and chromium to steel, the better the quality. Stainless steel is also a nonporous material, which means you can cook anything in it without any chemical reactions. By itself, though, stainless steel is a very poor conductor, and because of this, it is generally combined with aluminum, in some cases in a tri-ply fashion (i.e., steel, aluminum, steel) giving all the convenience of easy cleaning as well as good heat conduction.

Construction.

Now that we have explored the basic metals involved, let's take a look at construction. In order to be efficient and serviceable, a pot or pan must have these qualities:

1. It must have a strong, dentproof bottom. This is not hard to understand if you remember that the function of the pan is to transmit heat. A warped or dented pan will not absorb evenly, particularly on an electric stove. This will cause the bottom of the pan to have hot spots and may result in food burned to the pan, or a curdled sauce.

2. It must be well balanced to assure that it remains flat on the cooking surface and is not too difficult to handle when filled.

3. The handle must be secured to the pan in such a way as to achieve the maximum of balance and strength. Welding is the most durable method.

4. The handle should be heat resistant. Wooden handles have always been the best for this, but they do not take prolonged moisture well. The new treated compressed wood materials, or laminated wood, are ideal.

5. The lid should fit securely. It should be made of the same gauge material as the pan, and it should have a heat-resistant knob, or handle. The purpose of a lid is to seal in the moisture of the food yet allow trapped steam to escape, lest the pan become a pressure cooker.

Basic Requirements.

Now that you know what metal you want in your pots and pans and how you want them designed, your next decision concerns what you need for your own kitchen. Don't make the mistake of equipping your kitchen for its storage capacity, rather than for your cooking capacity. You will find that professional equipment stores and stacks well and has a multiplicity of uses. I have seen some incredibly small restaurant kitchens turn out an astounding number of great meals with seemingly a minimum of effort. You will discover that when you have several great skillets, all-purpose sauce-pans and a heavy-duty stockpot, your versatility is unlimited.

This is my basic list of the minimum number of pots and pans you will need to get your kitchen operating well:

5-quart sautéing pan with straight sides, a long handle on one side and a short handle on the other so that it is easy to lift.
5-quart combination sautéing pan and casserole with straight sides, two short handles so that it can be used in the oven.
1½-quart saucepan
2-quart saucepan

two 3-quart saucepans
5-quart steamer that can also be used as a stockpot, for cooking spaghetti, etc.
6- or 8-inch frying pan coated with Teflon or T-Fal, etc., for crêpes, omelettes or other egg cookery
Pyrex double boiler

I recommend that you also purchase lids for each of these because it makes them much more versatile.

Knives

There is nothing a professional chef prizes more than his knives, and for good reason: no single tool is more important in the preparation of food. A dull knife makes you an inefficient workman, a dull knife wastes a great deal of time, and a dull knife is dangerous. If you are a serious cook, you must have professional knives, and you must treat them with loving care.

When you buy a knife, think of it as a precision tool. Knives are designed to perform specific functions and will be more efficient if you use them that way. But first you must learn to select a good knife. This is not always easy, because poor knives and good knives often look alike. The most important test is how well its blade will take and hold an edge. To do this well, the knife must be made of high-quality steel, it must be tempered accurately to obtain the perfect degree of hardness, and the grinding of the blade must be done skillfully. The steel should have a satiny rather than a mirror polish, indicating a hand finish.

For many years, the most popular knives among the professionals were made of high-carbon steel. (Carbon is found to some degree in all steel knives because it provides hardness and contributes to the tempering process.) Carbon-steel knives take a very sharp edge, lose it quickly, but are easy to resharpen with a butcher's steel. My main objection to carbon steel is that the surface tarnishes, rusts, and reacts poorly to all acidic food. Ordinary stainless-steel knives, on the other hand, are much easier to clean and maintain; they hold an edge longer but are almost impossible to sharpen by hand.

If you could look at the cutting edge of a professional's knife under a microscope, you'd see what look like tiny saw teeth. These are what give "bite" to the cutting action, but with use and abuse (like throwing your knives in a drawer), they tend to bend. Maintaining an edge is similar to an orthodontist straightening teeth. The best tool for this purpose is a butcher's sharpening steel. It resets rather than files the edge, and employing a butcher's steel before every use is good practice.

Certain food acids can stain even the most stainless of steels, so it's good practice to wipe a knife with a damp cloth after every use. Do not put your knives into a sink of sudsy water. You may cut yourself in trying to retrieve them.

Also, no matter what the manufacturer says, do not ever put knives into a dishwasher, as the edges can bang against other cutlery or silverware. Store your knives in a specially designed stand or put them in your drawer on top of a magnetic strip so that they do not slide around. Don't put a bunch of junk on top of them. Also remind your family that they are not screwdrivers! With this care your knives will serve you for a lifetime.

An efficient kitchen must have the right selection of knives. All knives are designed by the cut of the blade to do certain jobs, in much the same way as are woodworking tools.

I suggest that you buy the following knives. They will handle any job you can come up with.

3-inch paring knife
4-inch paring knife
6-inch utility knife
10-inch slicer—for slicing your roasts
8- or 10-inch cook's knife—for chopping
10-inch knife with serrated edge—for bread, tomatoes, etc.

And of course, you must buy a butcher's steel, preferably made by the same company that made your knives.

A large fork for holding your roasts for slicing should also be in your house. Forks are generally made by the same companies that manufacture knives.

How to Use a Butcher's Sharpening Steel

1. Hold the steel firmly in your left hand with the guard positioned to stop the knife blade, should it ever slip.
2. Hold the knife in your right hand and place on top of the steel as shown.
3. Raise back of blade ⅛ inch.
4. Now, moving the blade only, draw it across the steel in an arching curve pivoted at your wrist. The blade tip should leave the steel about two-thirds of the way down.
5. Repeat the same action with the blade on the bottom side of the steel.
6. Alternate top and bottom five or six times. For best results, imagine that you're using the knife to shave the grooves off the steel.

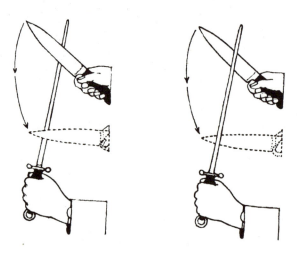

Basic Cookware for the Oven

Generally speaking, it is much more difficult to make a mistake in choosing pans for your oven than for surface cooking. This is not too hard to understand if you remember that the function of ovenware is to retain heat, not transmit it. That, of course, is why glass is satisfactory for much baking. Most professionals prefer aluminum, however, and I tend to agree, with one exception. I much prefer stainless steel roasting pans because they are much easier to clean.

Your minimum ovenware requirements should be:

2 heavy stainless-steel roasting pans, one 12 inches in length to accommodate a small roast and one 18 inches long to roast your biggest turkey

stainless-steel or nickel-plated adjustable rack that will fit both pans. Stay away from other materials; they are just too hard to clean.

heavy aluminum jelly-roll pan—Stay away from cheap, lightweight ones, as they bend out of shape too easily and warp in high heat.

10-inch springform pan, or 2 layer-cake pans if you prefer

2 cookie sheets of heavy-gauge aluminum or stainless steel

10-inch ovenproof china quiche pan—I like them better than the traditional metal ones, which are generally too low, because I like a thick custard. Also, you can bring the china one to the table.

2 Pyrex loaf pans for making bread, pâté or meat loaf—I prefer the ovenproof glass, as it is much easier to clean and bakes as well as metal.

au gratin dish—These come in various sizes to suit your needs. They are excellent for dishes that need to be browned under a broiler or for oven baking. They are made from various materials: copper, stainless steel, ovenproof china or ovenproof pottery.

1½-quart soufflé dish made from ovenproof and freezerproof glass. I find these the best, since they can be used not only for soufflés but for small salads, fruits, chocolate mousse, etc. Make certain that the glass can be put into the freezer. Manufacturers generally specify this. The best ones are made from industrial glass by Jena in Germany or Kimax in America. Make sure that the dish has straight sides at least 2 inches down so that you can put a collar on it for frozen soufflés.

muffin pan made from heavy aluminum or heavy-gauge tinned steel

aluminum or ovenproof-glass ring mold, which has a myriad of uses in making hot and cold dishes, such as mousse, custard, Bavarian cream, etc.

2 round metal cake racks for cooling cakes, cookies, etc.

Indispensable Tools

Most kitchen drawers are filled with accumulated gadgets and gimmicks that have no purpose except to take up space. I suggest you throw them away or have a garage sale. Your kitchen is your workshop and should contain only basic tools, and those should be at your fingertips. The following is a list of the things every kitchen should have. In fact, it is also the same list of tools I take when I travel all over the country doing cooking classes.

3 stainless-steel bowls (at least)—These sometimes come in a set or can be bought individually in the sizes that suit your needs best.

set of 4 wooden spoons—I prefer the spatula-shaped ones made from boxwood, which is the finest quality wood available. Although they are more expensive, they are well worth the investment. They always stay smooth and generally have a much longer life than cheaper spoons. Don't ever put a wooden spoon into a dishwasher, as it will invariably dry out and break. Simply wash in detergent, rinse well and dry.

2 large stainless-steel spoons, one with holes and one without. Their uses are unlimited.

large stainless-steel tongs to turn your meats when sautéing or to remove food from hot oil. Make sure they are about 12 inches long; the shorter ones defeat the whole purpose of keeping your hands away from the hot oil. I prefer the U-shaped rather than the scissor type.

2 spatulas, a small one (4 inch) for turning and moving smaller items, such as eggs, and a large one (7 inch) for whole cakes, fish or for transferring your carved meat from the carving board to the serving platter. Make sure they are made from stainless steel rather than carbon steel.

stainless-steel bulb baster for basting your roasts. Forget about plastic or glass ones. They are both impractical. You can buy a brush for cleaning your baster, or if you put it into a dishwasher, make sure you remove the suction bulb and wash it by hand; otherwise it will deteriorate very quickly.

1 large and 1 small rubber spatula—They have no equal for scraping bowls or folding foods together.

pair of scissors—All-purpose stainless-steel kitchen scissors can be used for anything, including cutting poultry.

vegetable peeler made from stainless steel to resist rust. You can, by the way, keep the peeler sharp with your butcher's steel.

four-sided stainless-steel grater for the jobs that are too small for a food processor or, even more essential, when you don't have one.

large stainless-steel colander for straining spaghetti, washing fruits, salads, etc.

1 small (3½-inch) and 1 large (7¼-inch) strainer made from stainless steel, with a fine mesh to trap even the tiniest food particles. The strainer should form a bowl, with an upstanding stainless-steel rim and hook welded to one side so that it can rest securely on the rim of another vessel.

garlic press—a well-made, large rectangular garlic press. They now come "self-cleaning" which eliminates a great deal of pain.

small whisk made from stainless steel. It will stand between you and lumps in your sauce. Make sure it is well balanced so that it is not awkward to handle and is the larger balloon type. (If you do not have a good electric mixer, get yourself a large whisk, too.)

set of measuring cups made from stainless steel. You can measure dry ingredients accurately by filling cups and leveling off with a knife. They come in a set of four that has ¼, ⅓, ½ and 1 cup sizes.

set of measuring spoons—They should be clearly marked ¼ teaspoon, ½ teaspoon, 1 teaspoon and 1 tablespoon. Here again I prefer stainless.

3 measuring cups (liquids)—These should be made of transparent ovenproof glass. They are now marked in metric measures as well as cups. I suggest you have a 1-cup, 2-cup and 4-cup size.

thermometers—A meat thermometer of good quality is especially helpful when you just start cooking and aren't yet quite sure of cooking times. Select one of the ones with a thinner rod so that it doesn't make big holes in your meat. I also find it's a good idea to test your oven frequently with an *oven thermometer*. Ovens do change, and accurate temperatures are essential for good baking. A *deep-frying thermometer* is handy unless you have an electric fryer—which is not a bad idea—and can be used as a candy thermometer when heating sugar.

pepper mill—It is definitely important to have a good one of these since there is no substitute for freshly ground pepper. Prepackaged ground pepper is awful. (In addition to my small hand grinder, with which I travel, I have a small electric coffee grinder at home that I use to grind pepper. It lets me grind from very fine to very coarse with the flip of a switch. This is definitely not necessary. It's for the cook who has everything.)

wooden cutting board—It is essential to have a good one of these (unless you have one built into your kitchen counter already). It should be at least 1 inch thick. There are also new plastic ones, which I use only when traveling since I don't consider them very good. Strangely enough, they are more difficult to clean than wood. They also get very tacky looking after a while. As for hygiene, believe me, with proper care, wood is much cleaner. Besides, cooks have been using wooden cutting boards for the last couple of hundred years at least, and I never knew anyone who died from using one.

lemon zester—A most ingenious little tool for producing lemon, orange or lime peel without the pain of a grater and without cutting too deeply, which adds the white bitter pith to the peel—definitely a must in my kitchen.

pastry scraper made from stainless steel. Not only is it an invaluable tool when baking, it is great to pick up chopped foods without spilling them all over the place. I also use mine for cleaning my wooden boards.

14-inch pastry bag—I find the flexible nylon ones the most practical, not only for handling, but also because they are easy to clean with soap and water and dry very fast. Stay away from cotton ones. They start to smell awful after a while.

set of pastry tubes—A full set of twelve tinned steel pastry tubes, which can be used for all decorating or for making cream puffs, etc.

rolling pin—I prefer the French-style tapered rolling pin since it is easier to use and quite sufficient except if you intend to make puff pastry. In that case, you will need a very heavy ball-bearing type pin.

soup ladle made from stainless steel. As the name implies, it is for dishing out soups and other liquids. I find a 6- or 8-ounce ladle the best size.

small spatula made from stainless steel, with a laminated wood handle. (This and the next item are my favorite tools for turning crêpes, omelettes, etc. I surely would be lost without them.)

small 3-pronged fork—I stir a lot of things with it, mix my omelettes, or pick up foods—a must in every kitchen.

ball of cotton twine for tying up the paper collar on your cold soufflé or tying up that leg of lamb. And, of course, without it you can't truss your chicken.

parchment paper—Although this isn't a tool, it is necessary to have when making a jelly roll or cooking en papillote.

can opener—As far as I am concerned, the only one worth having is the gear-driven Swing-A-Way. Made of stainless steel with easy-to-grip handles covered with plastic, it can be easily washed. There are also electric openers with heads easily removable for washing; so if you must have an electric one, be sure to buy one of those.

funnel—Buy an all-purpose funnel made from stainless steel. It should be 3 inches across the top and ½ inch at the bottom tip. Very handy to have around.

scale—If you get into baking, I definitely recommend that you buy a good-quality scale. A beam-balance scale is the best. You use it by sliding two weights along the calibrated double beam. Scales are generally marked both in grams and ounces, and should have a removable tray for easy cleaning.

pastry brush—Again, if you are into baking, get a good small (1-inch) pastry brush made from undyed hog bristles. The bristles must be attached to the handle as securely as possible to prevent shedding. Wash the brush under running water immediately after each use and dry in the air.

dredger—This is the most efficient way to sprinkle powdered sugar over your crêpes, etc. It looks like a large salt shaker, but has larger holes in the cap and a handle on the side.

screwpull or corkscrew for opening bottles of wine.

Laborsaving Devices

There are many jobs in the kitchen that are both exhausting and tedious. I refer to such things as pureeing fruits and vegetables, mixing cake batter, creaming butter, beating egg whites, and more. If you attempt to do these jobs by hand, you will wear down both your strength and your enthusiasm. Regardless of what some cookbooks may tell you, all these jobs can be done better by machine. If you want to be a good cook in this fast, modern world of ours, you must learn to conserve your time and energy for creative jobs.

Whenever you buy an electrical appliance, always choose the very best of its kind. If you buy a cheap appliance, you will only find you have to replace it later. As my mother always taught me, "You only get what you pay for."

If you are, or intend to become, a dedicated cook, I strongly recommend you buy a heavy-duty mixer. For many years, KitchenAid has dominated this field, but I am happy to report that the Kenwood mixers from England are now available here. The Kenwood Major model I consider the best-designed and most functional mixer as well as the most powerful available for home use. It has a 7-quart stainless-steel bowl in which you can beat two eggs as easily as twelve, or whip cream or knead bread. It has many other attachments, but the one I like best is the large blender. This will save you a lot of counter space. Never buy an appliance you can't keep on the counter. You will find you'll never use it.

I am sure that by now everyone has heard of the food processor. I had one of the first brought into this country by Carl Sontheimer, President of Cuisinart. This machine certainly has created a small revolution in home cooking. There are certain jobs, such as making salmon mousse or mayonnaise, for which it has no peer, but I caution you against the belief that a food processor will make you an instant chef.

Cuisinart makes a very high-quality machine, but each of its succeeding models has become more expensive. I have all of them and find the original one as good as any.

If you like fresh orange juice, as I do, or you cook with fruit juice, I suggest you own an electric citrus juicer. I recommend the Braun citrus juicer because it is the best designed and easiest to clean.

Tips on Cooking Items

I am a great believer in using the best ingredients in cooking. The old saying, "You only get out what you put in," certainly holds true, so here are tips about some of the ingredients that are used in this cookbook. Of course there are hundreds more, but you have to start somewhere.

Stocks.

Whenever possible, I use homemade ones. If I buy canned stocks, I use the double-strength kind, because then I can water them down or use them full-strength when more flavor is needed. They are quite salty, so do make adjustments in your seasoning.

Butter and Oils.

I use unsalted butter exclusively in my house since it does not interfere with the flavors, and I can keep it in the freezer to retain freshness when buying a larger amount. (I am all for sales when it is the brand I like.) As to oils, use whichever type you prefer. I generally use corn, sunflower or safflower oil for cooking. For flavoring, such as in salad dressings, the sky is the limit: hazelnut, walnut, extra virgin olive oil are all good. I don't generally use margarine in cooking anymore. It is simply vegetable oil that went through the hydrogenating process; so when the recipe calls for melting, why not use oil to start with? But, of course, that is only a personal choice. You use whatever you like.

Cheese.

When you use cheese in cooking, you must remember it is an ingredient that greatly influences the flavor of a dish. I caution you to use only authentic, high-quality cheeses. Otherwise you can destroy delicate flavors. The two most commonly used cheeses in cooking are Switzerland, not Swiss, and Parmesan. There is very little similarity between what is sold in this country as Swiss cheese and true Switzerland cheese, except for the holes. When you buy it, look for the word Switzerland stenciled all over the rind. The same is true of Parmesan cheese. The products sold here in jars as grated Parmesan are generally very far from the real thing. I suggest you buy a small piece of aged imported Parmesan from a reputable dealer and keep it tightly wrapped in your refrigerator. Grate it freshly as you need it, or let the shop grate it, and freeze whatever you don't need immediately.

Chocolate.

Most beginners find chocolate the hardest of all foods to handle. Until you learn the ropes, it can be difficult. Chocolate must be melted without any liquid at all, or with at least two tablespoons of liquid for every ounce of chocolate. In the latter case, any lesser amount of liquid, even a tiny drop spilled in a pan of melting chocolate, will turn it into a sticky mess that cannot even be stirred. If this happens to you, the chocolate can be saved by the addition of vegetable shortening. However, I much prefer to melt chocolate in liquid, either rum or coffee, although milk or water will do as well. Just make sure you use enough liquid. Melt chocolate over low heat, stirring constantly, because it scorches very easily. Again, make sure to get good chocolate.

Gelatin.

There is more confusion about how to dissolve gelatin than almost anything else in cooking. It used to be that the Knox gelatin people put the how-to on each envelope of gelatin. Well, no more, so here is the proper way to dissolve gelatin before putting it into a cold mixture.

Fill a 1-cup Pyrex measuring cup one-quarter full of cold water. Sprinkle a package of unflavored gelatin into the water. Stir with a spoon and allow the gelatin to soften. Place the Pyrex cup into a shallow pan of boiling water until the gelatin is completely liquid, then remove the cup from the pan and set aside to cool.

Heavy Cream.

Although I am not the "crusader" type, I would like everyone in this country to be aware of what the dairy industry has done to the supply of heavy, or whipping, cream. With few exceptions, you will no longer find fresh heavy cream at your grocer's. What you will find is ultrapasteurized cream. This means that the dairies have heated the cream to a temperature that will kill the natural bacteria, thereby lengthening the shelf life of the cream. This is just great for the dairies and for your grocer. But it is just awful for the consumer. This new version of heavy cream tastes terrible. It does not whip well, and to make matters worse, once you open the container the ultra-pasteurized cream keeps no longer than fresh cream. (To add insult to injury they haven't even lowered the price!)

I strongly urge you to protest wherever you can. In some states the dairy industry has gotten legislation passed to ban the sale of fresh heavy cream using the specious argument that it is not safe. I'll give you an example of how transparent this fraud actually is. We recently catered desserts for a very large restaurant for over a month. They were being supplied with ultrapasteurized cream by one of the largest dairies in the New York/New Jersey area. We refused to use it. The food buyer for the restaurant was told by his dairy that they no longer sold fresh cream. We made the buyer cancel his order for cream, 50 to 100 quarts a day, so we could order from our dairy. Within two hours of that cancellation, the sales manager of the buyer's dairy was at the door with 100 quarts of fresh cream. He said it was all a misunderstanding. I can assure you that unless consumers take action, you won't find a drop of fresh cream anywhere before too long.

Eggs.

Open a carton of eggs. You will see that all the eggs are packed with the pointed side down and the rounded side up. There is an air space between the egg white and the shell on the rounded side. Many times when you boil an egg, particularly right from the refrigerator, the shell will crack. To avoid this, you need only make a small hole in the rounded side with a pin to release the air pressure. Be careful not to make the tiny hole too deep; go just past the shell; otherwise you will puncture the egg white.

Some hints about eggs:

1. Eggshells absorb odors readily. Store eggs away from strong-smelling foods.
2. Don't overcook hard-boiled eggs. My method is to put the eggs in cold water in a saucepan, bring to a boil, then cut down the heat and simmer for 2 minutes. Then turn off the heat and let eggs sit in the water for an additional 10 minutes. Rinse off with cold water and peel. When you see a gray film between the yolk and the white, you have overcooked the eggs.
3. The reason why some hard-boiled eggs are hard to peel is that they are too fresh. Eggs are best for boiling when they are at least two to three days old.
4. Eggs in the refrigerator will stay fresh enough for soft-boiling for up to eight days and for baking up to a month.
5. When the egg yolk is not in the middle of the white it means your eggs weren't very fresh. The color of the yolk has nothing to do with freshness. It reflects what the chicken was fed.

Herbs and Spices.

Many herbs are available in fresh form the year round and some only seasonally. Discuss this with your greengrocer and buy the fresh herbs whenever they are available. If you have a supply of fresh herbs you wish to preserve, do the following. Place a small amount of the herb in each section of an ice-cube tray. Fill the tray with water and freeze. Remove the cubes one by one as you need the herbs.

Whenever you use dried herbs, rub them between the palms of your hands to release the flavor. Always break a bay leaf in half, and remember to remove it from food before serving. Dried herbs and spices lose their flavor when not stored properly. If you keep them in airtight jars away from strong light, they will last for about 1 to 1½ years.

Since the purpose of herbs and spices is to enhance the flavor in your food, make sure you buy only the best quality. When storing herbs, put them inside a cabinet on one of those lazy-Susan stands and line them up alphabetically so you can find them more easily. Paprika and curry powder should be stored in the refrigerator for best shelf life.

Lemons.

When you buy lemons, store them outside the refrigerator until fully ripe. You will find them easier to squeeze and you will get a lot more juice from them. When you need the juice of only one lemon, don't bother with your squeezer and strainer. Just squeeze it in the palm of your hand and let your fingers act as a strainer. Avoid this method, though, when you have a cut in your hand. It smarts.

Salt and Pepper.

The two most frequently used seasonings should be used and selected with care. I generally prefer sea salt for its more delicate flavor. To grind your salt freshly is nonsense, since the only people benefiting from this are the people who make salt grinders. I generally use less salt than most people. Because of this, you will seldom find a measure for it in my recipes. As the amount used is a matter of individual taste, I always keep salt on the table for those who prefer more than I do.

Pepper is another story. Not to use a pepper mill to grind your pepper freshly is like keeping your perfume bottle open. The minute pepper is ground it starts losing its flavor, which means when you buy already ground pepper, most of the flavor has evaporated. My favorite is the Telicherry peppercorns, which are of particularly fine quality. I personally do not use white peppercorns, as they lack the robust flavor of the black ones.

Green Peppercorns.

Ah, the joy of it—definitely the ultimate in pepper flavor. Green peppercorns are those that have been picked before fully ripe and then either packed in water or freeze-dried. (They also come packed in vinegar—don't buy them, they're awful.) Green peppercorns have a distinctive taste, smoother than black pepper, that doesn't burn your tongue—it simply makes your tastebuds come alive. Try them in the recipe for Tournedos Madagascar or use them next time you make steak au poivre. The chances are you'll get hooked on them. Once you've opened the can (if they're packed in water), put the ones you don't use in a dish. Cover them with water and put them into the freezer. If you have a large can, put them by the tablespoonful into your ice-cube tray, cover with water and freeze. When frozen, store the cubes in a plastic bag, and next time you need them, just pop the cubes in your sauce. Voilà!

Rice.

Our two most commonly used rices are white and converted. Both of these rices have been stripped of the outer brown coating, but the converted rice has been enriched to replace the nutrients lost in stripping away the outer coat. I find Uncle Ben's Converted Rice and Carolina Enriched Rice excellent products.

Brown rice, or natural rice, has a great many more nutrients than white. It also has a delicious nutty flavor not found in white rice. It requires a little longer cooking time, but I recommend you try it. Be careful—it has a much shorter shelf life and may spoil.

Vegetables.

Make it a point to find a store where you can buy fresh vegetables when they are in season. The difference between freshly picked vegetables and those even one day old is incredible. Most of us are not lucky enough to live close to a source of freshly picked vegetables, but every day counts. If you can find a good reliable roadside market in the summer, by all means use it. Your state agricultural department can probably give you the names of the best markets in your area.

In most large cities, the vegetables are shipped under refrigeration and are at least four to five days old. When you can't find fresh vegetables that please you, frozen are better. I have never found good fresh peas in New York City, so I always use frozen.

When you get your fresh vegetables and salad greens home, always wash them thoroughly under cold water. Then dry them well, wrap in a few paper towels, enclose in a plastic bag and refrigerate. This will keep them crisp and fresh much longer.

Parsley.

To store, remove any yellow leaves and then wash the parsley well under cold water. Shake off excess moisture and wrap in a double layer of paper towels. Put into a plastic bag and store in the refrigerator. This will keep your parsley fresh and crisp for at least one week.

Never try to chop parsley when it is wet. It is not only difficult, but also the parsley becomes too soggy for decoration. You can chop parsley several days ahead and keep it in a closed container along with a paper towel to absorb excess moisture and prevent mold.

Asparagus.

Asparagus is one vegetable you should buy only when it is in season in your part of the country. Sadly enough, this is a very short time in most areas. When it is fresh from New Jersey, I eat it as much as I possibly can because the season is so short. We do get some rather beautiful asparagus from California, but the travel time is crucial.

When buying asparagus, look for these signs of freshness: stalks that are firm and tips that are closed. Avoid angular or flat stalks with large portions of white, which may be woody, and check the bottom of the stalks for dryness. The thickness of the stalk has nothing to do with freshness or tenderness. Use asparagus as soon as possible, but when storing it, keep in a tightly closed plastic bag in the refrigerator. I always peel asparagus because the skin is slightly bitter, and peeling makes it look a lot more attractive. And I cut off any woody part at the bottoms of the stalks, rather than breaking it off.

Broccoli.

When choosing broccoli, make sure it is firm, compact, and has closed bud-clusters of dark green. The stems should not be too thick, meaning it was not picked young enough, or dried out on the bottom. Enlarged or open buds and yellow wilted leaves indicate old age. Keep broccoli refrigerated in a plastic bag until used. Do not cook a whole head of broccoli without cutting off the florets and without cutting the stems and slicing them diagonally. Otherwise, by the time the stems are tender, the top will be overcooked.

Mushrooms.

When buying fresh mushrooms, choose ones that are white and firm to the touch. The skin between the cap and stem should be closed. The older the mushrooms, the more open they are. The lamellae under the cap should be a light beige; again, the darker they are, the older the mushrooms. To store, put into a plastic bag with several paper towels. (Mushrooms contain a great deal of moisture, which the paper towels will absorb.) Otherwise, they'll get wet and deteriorate faster. So stored, they will stay fresh for several days. Or you may freeze them. I've found the best method to do this is to slice the mushrooms and sauté in a little butter, then freeze them. Otherwise they lose too much flavor and texture. When fresh mushrooms are unavailable, buy freeze-dried ones, which are quite good. Stay away from canned mushrooms—they're awful!

Wine.

When you cook with wine or any other spirit, always remember that the rule is: if it isn't good enough to drink, it isn't good enough to eat. Since the alcohol evaporates in cooking, the main thing left is the flavor, which is why you added the wine in the first place. In the concentration of cooking down, if you start off with an inferior wine, the flavor only gets worse.

Once you open wine, whether it be red or white, make sure to refrigerate it. If you only have a quarter of a bottle left, transfer it into a smaller one, since what spoils wine is the air between it and the bottle opening.

Mustards.

The varieties of mustards available seem endless, and I never tire of trying a new one. When I went shopping the other day in one of the specialty stores, I counted thirty-five different varieties of mustard on the shelves. But by far one of my favorites is Pommery mustard. Its crushed mustard seeds and delicate seasoning makes it so delicious that one can almost eat it with a spoon. (My daughter, who is not yet one of the adventurous eaters, insists on having it with her hot dogs or in salad dressings, so I figure there is still hope for her.) My other favorite for cooking is Grey Poupon Dijon mustard. Originally made in Dijon, France, it is now produced in this country and is probably the best all-purpose mustard for salad dressings, mayonnaise, etc., you can find in any supermarket. Then there is dry mustard—I like Coleman's—which is very hot and must be used sparingly.

Vinegars.

You can buy a bottle of vinegar for 49 cents up to $10. What's the difference? Flavor. It comes in almost any imaginable flavor you want. I used to have at least four different ones on my shelf. Now I have one, cider vinegar, which I use for everything. If you like different flavors in your vinegar, why not make your own? It's a lot cheaper and more fun. Heat the vinegar, add a few sprigs of tarragon, or some shallots and garlic, put on a bamboo skewer. Or how about a piece of fresh ginger. The possibilities are limited only by your imagination.

Bread Crumbs.

Next time you have leftover French or Italian bread, slice it up, put overnight in the oven if you have a pilot light, or keep oven on at the lowest possible temperature for several hours. Just make sure that the bread is really dry or your bread crumbs will mildew. When dry, put the slices either in your blender or food processor and grind finely. You now have bread crumbs that will last for a long time.

When buying commercial bread crumbs, keep in mind that bread doesn't taste any better crumbled up than it does in slices, so buy them from a company that makes good bread to start with.

Vanilla.

I feel that most of you know all about my vanilla jar, but there are enough letters coming in with questions to merit repeating it one more time. Here it is!

I feel strongly about vanilla and—once you have tasted the difference between the real thing and the artificial one—I am convinced so will you. The finest vanilla beans grow in Madagascar, an island off the coast of Africa in the Indian Ocean. Vanilla beans are the seed shoots of an orchid. They look like long green beans when harvested. They are dried in the sun and cured. Their essence lies within the bean in the seeds, the thousands of little specks you see in real vanilla ice cream. It used to be quite bothersome to get at them; that is, if you didn't have a vanilla jar going. You take vanilla beans, put them into a glass jar and cover them completely with vodka. Buy the least expensive vodka for this since you are only interested in the alcohol content. After the beans have been soaking for about four to five days, you can then snip off the bottom of the bean with a knife—the thicker end, not the slightly bent end. Take two fingers and simply squeeze out the vanilla seeds, using half the beans or whatever your recipe calls for. Then put the beans back into the jar. When they are completely empty of seeds I put them in upside down so I don't keep squeezing without results. After your beans have been in the vodka for about six to eight weeks you can then use the liquid. (This depends, of course, on how many beans you have in there. One or two aren't going to do it. I recommend you start with fifteen.) At this point, the liquid is pure vanilla extract. When you have used about half of it, refill the jar with more vodka. You can tell there is no more flavor in your beans when the liquid doesn't turn dark anymore, but this takes a few years. I consider making your own vanilla extract the ultimate in perfection, and a vanilla jar probably will be the biggest conversation piece in your kitchen. I gave them as Christmas presents a few years ago to some friends and they were a big hit. I also put one or two vanilla beans in my jar of powdered sugar. This way, when I whip heavy cream for decorating or to go with strawberries, I only have to add sugar since it is already vanilla flavored.

Make sure to leave the beans in the jar all the time, because once you remove them the vanilla flavor will disappear since it is a very fragile fragrance. This is why all commercial vanilla sugar is made with artificial vanillin—it is more stable. But it also tastes *yech*.

First Courses and Appetizers

These days, a lot of people ask me for ideas about what to serve with drinks, about light food for a brunch or a Sunday-night supper, or just how to get away from the old routine hors d'oeuvres.

So in this chapter, I am going to give you my ideas for light dishes that can be served at an informal party. They are all comfortably eaten buffet-style, with only a fork and napkin. All of them also make elegant first courses for a more formal dinner.

Gravlax with Mustard Sauce

This is a very elegant and easy recipe to prepare. It is, of course, from Scandinavia, where they have made preparing fish the highest form of art.

2-pound piece of salmon, cut from the center section of the fish with the backbone and all small bones removed

3 tablespoons coarse salt (kosher)

4 tablespoons sugar

1 tablespoon coarsely ground black pepper

1 large bunch of fresh dill

Mix the salt, pepper and sugar together in a small bowl. Place the fish skin-side down on your counter. Rub the salt mixture well into the fish. Wash and dry the dill and place it on the fish. Close fish over dill like a sandwich.

Place the fish in a plastic bag and seal. Put the bag in the refrigerator and weight it down. Large cans of food are ideal for this. Refrigerate for at least 28 hours. The longer the better, up to 4 days. Remove weights and turn the fish about every 8 to 10 hours during that time.

When the salmon is cured (finished), remove it from the bag, scrape away the dill and seasoning and pat dry with paper towels. Place skin-side down, on a carving board and slice the salmon thinly on the diagonal, separating each slice from the skin. Serve with Mustard Sauce and thin slices of dark bread.

Yield: 8 servings as a first course or 16 servings as hors d'oeuvres

Mustard Sauce:

3   tablespoons Dijon-style or Pommery mustard

1   tablespoon sugar

2   tablespoons cider vinegar

¼   teaspoon salt

1   tablespoon finely chopped fresh dill

⅓   cup vegetable oil

Mix ingredients in a bowl or blender until well combined.

Yield: 1 cup

Salmon Supreme

3   salmon steaks, about 1-inch thick

Juice of 1 lemon

2   tablespoons chopped dill

1   package phyllo dough

8   tablespoons melted butter combined with

1   tablespoon Pommery mustard

Salt and pepper to taste

2   scallions, finely chopped

1   egg yolk mixed with

2   tablespoons milk

Skin and bone the salmon steaks (reserving skin and bones for stock); then cut in half and sprinkle with lemon juice and dill. Let marinate for about 5 minutes, then unroll phyllo dough. Brush the top sheet with the butter-mustard mixture and put one piece of salmon on the end of the dough. Season with salt and pepper and sprinkle some of the chopped scallions on top. Roll salmon in the pastry, folding in the sides. Repeat with the other two steaks.

Put them on a buttered cookie sheet and brush with the egg yolk-milk mixture. Bake in preheated 400°F. oven for 15 to 20 minutes or until golden brown.

Yield: 6 servings
Serve with Dill Sauce.

Dill Sauce:

4   tablespoons butter

4   tablespoons all-purpose flour

1½   cups fish stock

½   cup heavy cream

2   tablespoons chopped dill

Salt and pepper to taste

In a heavy stainless-steel or enamelware saucepan, melt the butter. Stir in flour over moderate heat. When mixture begins to bubble, stir and cook for another minute. Add fish stock and stir with a wire whisk until mixture begins to thicken and comes to a boil. Reduce heat, simmer for 2 minutes, stirring constantly, and add the cream and seasonings.

Yield: 2 cups

Note: To make fish stock, put the bones and skin from your salmon in a saucepan. Add 1 cup water and 1 cup dry white wine, 2 sprigs dill, ½ onion and 2 peppercorns. Bring to a boil and simmer for 15 minutes. Strain. *Yield: 2 cups*

Mussels in Mustard Sauce

Now that mussels are being farm raised, it is easier to get good ones. This is definitely one of my favorite dishes for lunch, along with a loaf of hot, crunchy French bread, a glass of white wine and a "thou." After you eat all the mussels, the best part is to dip the bread into the sauce and eat it.

3	*pounds mussels*
3	*tablespoons shallots, finely chopped*
1	*cup dry white wine*
2	*tablespoons Dijon-style mustard*
2	*tablespoons parsley, finely chopped*
½	*teaspoon thyme*
1	*clove garlic, put through garlic press*
	Salt and pepper to taste

Wash and clean the mussels. Put them into cold water and keep in cold water throughout the cleaning. Throw away all the open and broken mussels and any that are not firmly closed. Scrub the shells with a stiff brush and cut off the beard.

Put all ingredients except the mussels in a heavy sautéing pan, bring to a boil and simmer for 5 minutes. Then add the mussels, cover the pan and simmer for about 4 minutes, shaking the pan every so often.

Yield: 6 servings as first course or 4 servings as luncheon

Smoked Trout with Madeira Gelée and Horseradish Cream

This is a very elegant first course or luncheon, yet surprisingly simple to prepare. You will find the trout filets, smoked and skinned, in many fine "gourmet shops," or with one of the popular home smokers, you can do it yourself. For smoking trout, use hickory chips and add a few juniper berries. The horseradish sauce can also be served with smoked salmon. This is the same Madeira gelée I use for my Filet of Beef in Aspic.

½	*cup Madeira wine*
2	*packages unflavored gelatin*
2	*10½-ounce cans beef broth*
1	*can water*
6	*leaves of Boston lettuce*
6	*filets of smoked trout*

Put the Madeira in a Pyrex cup and sprinkle the gelatin over it. Place the cup in a shallow saucepan of boiling water and stir until gelatin is dissolved. Put the beef broth and water into a bowl, stir in the dissolved gelatin, cover bowl with plastic wrap and refrigerate until gelée is set.

Put the lettuce leaves on a platter or plates. Top with trout. Break up the set gelée with a kitchen knife and surround the trout with it. Serve Horseradish Cream on the side.

Yield: 6 servings

Horseradish Cream:

1 cup heavy cream,
  whipped to soft peaks

4 tablespoons white
  horseradish

  Dash of Tabasco

  Salt and pepper to taste

To make Horseradish Cream, simply combine all ingredients and refrigerate.

Yield: 1 cup

Lorna's Stuffed Grape Leaves

Several years ago I spent Thanksgiving with Dennis and his family. His brother Patrick learned an easier way to carve a turkey from me, and I learned from Patrick's wife how to make the best stuffed grape leaves I ever ate. They have been a staple in my house ever since, and I am sure they will be in yours.

1-quart jar vine
leaves (80 per jar,
Lorna uses Orlando
brand)

2 bunches scallions,
  finely chopped

2 tablespoons parsley,
  finely chopped

1½ cups olive oil

1½ cups raw rice (short-
  grain brown rice)

2 tablespoons freshly
  chopped dill

¾ cup pine nuts

⅔ cup seedless currants,
  soaked in

2 cups white wine

  Salt and pepper to
  taste

  Juice of 4 lemons

3 cups beef bouillon,
  fresh, or if canned,
  unconcentrated

2 cups water

Remove vine leaves from jar, scald them with hot water and drain. Cut off stems from leaves carefully, pat each leaf dry and place shiny-surface down on paper towels. In a skillet, sauté scallions and parsley in 4 teaspoons of the olive oil. Add the rice, dill, pine nuts, the currants with the wine, and salt and pepper.

Cover and simmer for 15 minutes. *(Note:* If brown rice is used, simmer for 25 minutes.) Rice will not be fully cooked at the end of this time. (Half a cup of water may be needed during the simmering, depending upon the rice.) Set aside and cool.

When cool, place 1 teaspoon of the rice mixture in the center of each leaf. Fold end of leaf over to cover filling. Fold up sides of leaf and roll over carefully until a cylinder, about 2 inches long, is formed.

Arrange the stuffed grape leaves in a heavy pot, sprinkle each layer with lemon juice and 2 teaspoons of olive oil. Pour bouillon plus the 2 cups water and the remaining olive oil and lemon juice over them. (Don't use quite all of the lemon juice, particularly if the lemons are large.)

Place a plate on top to weight the grape-leaf cylinders down, and simmer over a very low heat for 40 to 50 minutes. Remove, drain and cool before serving.

Yield: approximately 80

Antipasto

Whenever I get a chance to stay home and watch television I like to eat either Artichokes Vinaigrette—and I can eat three in the course of a good movie—or I make a platter of antipasto. Just around the corner from my school is a great Italian store where I will order some:

Prosciutto, paper-thin slices

Mozzarella, fresh

Genoa salami, thinly sliced

Pimiento

Hot Tuscan pepper

Black olives niçoise

Honeydew, perfectly ripened

A loaf of semolina bread

I arrange all the antipasto ingredients on a large platter and heat the bread in the oven. (If you ever have a chance to get semolina bread, try it—it's terrific.) I set all of this next to me and enjoy myself. Now, that's my idea of a TV snack.

Fettuccine Alfredo

I have always maintained that if you eat a dish that is high in calories, make sure it's worth it. Well, this dish certainly fits both categories, so make sure you don't eat it too often. It can be served either as a first course or as a complete meal, in which case I suggest you serve it with an arugula salad. Serve the fettuccine the minute you make it, as the sauce gets absorbed by the noodles fairly quickly. And of course I don't have to mention to you that the noodles should be cooked al dente.

6 *quarts water*

1 *tablespoon salt*

1 *pound fettuccine noodles (thin noodles ½-inch wide), packaged, homemade or fresh from an Italian store*

4 *ounces sweet butter (1 stick)*

In a large saucepan, bring the water and salt to a rolling boil and add the noodles. Cook 5 to 10 minutes, depending on the noodles. Fresh ones take considerably less time. When cooked but still firm (test by biting one), pour them into a colander. In the meantime, melt the butter in the saucepan, add the heavy cream, heat, then add the sour cream and stir over low heat. Do not let boil. Add the noodles, Parmesan cheese, chives, salt and pepper. Combine and serve.

Yield: 6 servings

1   cup heavy cream

1   cup sour cream

1   cup grated Parmesan cheese

½   cup fresh chives, finely cut

Salt and pepper to taste

Linguine with Pesto Sauce

I love every kind of pasta and make it for myself when it's easy. With a food processor, this recipe is a snap.

½   cup grated Parmesan cheese

½   cup pine nuts (also called pignolia)

3   cloves garlic, put through a garlic press

¼–½ cup olive oil (enough to give the sauce a thick consistency)

Handful of fresh basil leaves

Cooked linguine

Put all of these ingredients (except for the linguine, of course) in your food processor and process until smooth. Place on top of cooked linguine which is, of course, al dente, not mush. (See Linguine with Marinara Sauce for cooking directions.)

Yield: 1½ cups

Linguine with Marinara Sauce

½ cup olive oil

2 Bermuda onions, coarsely chopped

6 large cloves garlic, finely chopped

1 35-ounce can Italian plum tomatoes

1 6-ounce can tomato paste

1 10½-ounce can beef broth (Campbell's)

1 cup red wine

1 bay leaf

1 tablespoon dried sweet basil

1 teaspoon oregano

1 teaspoon thyme

Salt and pepper, lots of fresh pepper

2 pounds linguine

Heat the olive oil in a heavy sautéing pan and add the onions. Cook over high heat until the onions are very brown and almost crisp. At this point, they almost turn to sugar. Add the garlic and stir for about a minute. Then add all the rest of the ingredients. Lower the heat and simmer sauce for about 1½ hours. Make sure the sauce is bubbling gently during this time and, if necessary, add a little more red wine.

Yield: 4 cups

Cook the linguine as follows: Fill a large pot with water, add some salt and bring to a rolling boil. Put fresh or packaged linguine into the water, bring to a boil again and cook about 7 minutes, stirring with a wooden spoon. You don't need to add oil; the pasta won't stick together. Pour the water and linguine into a large colander in the sink to drain, and run very hot water over the pasta to rinse off the starch. Put the pot back on the stove over low heat, add a couple of tablespoons of butter to melt, lots of fresh pepper and then the drained linguine. Stir with the wooden spoon to coat the linguine well. Put it onto plates and spoon the Marinara Sauce over it. You can serve some freshly grated Parmesan cheese on the side, if you wish, and some garlic bread.

Yield: 8 servings

Hearts of Palm au Gratin

This makes a fabulous first course however you serve it—in one large dish or small individual gratin dishes. You can make it several hours ahead and then simply reheat at serving time.

1   can hearts of palm, drained and cut into chunks

6   hard-boiled eggs

6   slices of ham, about 1/4-inch thick, cut into strips

Butter

Grease a round or oval ovenproof dish with butter and put the hearts of palm in it. Cut the hard-boiled eggs into quarters and add them to the dish, then sprinkle the strips of ham on top. Cover with Mornay Sauce. Put under a preheated broiler for about 10 minutes or until lightly browned and bubbly. Sprinkle some parsley over top and serve.

Yield: 6 servings

Mornay Sauce:

4   tablespoons butter

4   tablespoons all-purpose flour

2   cups milk

1/2   cup grated Switzerland Swiss cheese

1/2   cup grated Parmesan cheese

Salt and pepper to taste

Chopped fresh parsley

To make the sauce, melt the butter in a heavy saucepan and stir in the flour. Cook for a few moments without browning, then add the milk, stirring constantly with a whisk until it comes to a boil in order to avoid lumps. Lower heat and simmer for 2 minutes. Add the Swiss cheese, Parmesan cheese and salt and pepper. Continue simmering until the Swiss cheese is melted. Turn off heat.

Artichokes Vinaigrette

This is definitely my favorite way of having fresh artichokes, whether I serve them as first course, lunch or my favorite snack while watching a good TV movie. I prefer serving the artichokes at room temperature rather than straight from the refrigerator.

6   *whole artichokes*
    Juice of 2 lemons
1   *tablespoon salt*

Slice off stem and top portion of each artichoke. With scissors, cut off points of each remaining whole leaf. Place artichokes side by side in a large saucepan, and fill pan with water just to top of the artichokes. Add lemon juice and salt, bring to a boil, cover and simmer for about 45 minutes, depending on the size of the artichokes. When outside leaves pull out easily, artichokes are done. Drain and allow to cool. Refrigerate, covered.

Note: You can also steam the artichokes. The cooking time is about the same. Make sure to check on your water. Since artichokes absorb a great deal, your pot may run dry and burn. (I know . . . it happened to me several times.)

Dressing:

2   *tablespoons Dijon-style mustard (Grey Poupon), or Pommery mustard*

½   *cup vegetable oil*

2   *tablespoons olive oil (Bertolli)*

3   *tablespoons cider vinegar*

1   *teaspoon honey*

1   *hard-boiled egg, put through a coarse strainer or very finely chopped*

2   *tablespoons parsley, finely chopped*

2   *tablespoons chopped pimiento*

To make the dressing, put the mustard, oils, vinegar and honey in your blender and blend for about 1 minute. Place in a bowl, stir in the rest of the ingredients and refrigerate until ready to use. Serve in small bowls for each person to dip their artichoke leaves into.

Yield: 6 servings

Cold Filled Artichoke Bottoms

This recipe makes a wonderful first course when you don't feel like having soup. The filling can also be used to stuff scooped-out tomatoes or avocados for a great lunch.

1	can artichoke bottoms
	Lemon juice
8	lettuce leaves

Open your can of artichoke bottoms, discard the brine, put the bottoms on a plate and sprinkle them with lemon juice. Cover them and put in the refrigerator to cool.

Dressing:

2	tablespoons mayonnaise
½	tablespoon curry powder
2	tablespoons vegetable oil
2	tablespoons cider vinegar
1	tablespoon chutney, if available
	Salt and pepper to taste

Put the ingredients for your dressing in a blender and blend until well combined.

Filling:

3	hard-boiled eggs, coarsely chopped
3	tablespoons chopped pimiento
3	tablespoons black olives, chopped
2	jars small shrimp
1	tablespoon chopped parsley
	Salt and pepper to taste

To make filling, take the eggs, pimiento, olives, shrimp and parsley, and put them into a bowl. Pour the dressing on top and mix all the ingredients well. Season with salt and freshly ground pepper. Chill in the refrigerator for 30 minutes.

Put one lettuce leaf on a salad plate, place one artichoke bottom on top and fill it with the curried shrimp salad. Do this with all eight of them, adding a little more parsley on top if desired, and serve.

Yield: 8 servings

Pâté Normandy

If you generally don't like chicken liver pâté, try this one. You will find its taste totally different. The addition of the calvados does wonderful things for the pâté.

2   tablespoons vegetable oil

2   tablespoons butter

1   onion, coarsely chopped

1   Granny Smith apple, peeled, cored and chopped

Salt and pepper to taste

½   teaspoon thyme

1   pound chicken livers, with all fat removed

4   tablespoons calvados (French apple brandy)

¼   pound sweet butter

Heat the vegetable oil and the 2 tablespoons butter in a heavy sautéing pan, add the onion, apple, salt and pepper and thyme, and sauté until lightly brown. Cover the pan and simmer until the apple is soft (about 3 minutes). Then remove this mixture from the pan and put aside. In the same pan, sauté the chicken livers, adding a little more butter if necessary, making sure not to overcook them. The livers should still be pink inside. Heat the calvados, set aflame and pour over the chicken livers. When the flame has died out, add the onion-apple mixture, stir well and let cool. Then put this mixture through the food processor, add the ¼ pound butter a tablespoon at a time and puree until smooth. Put into a dish and refrigerate for several hours before serving.

Yield: 14 to 16 servings as hors d'oeuvres

Roquefort Mousse with Fresh Pears

This makes a wonderful first course when made in small individual molds and surrounded by sliced fresh pears. (If they aren't ripe put them in a brown paper bag along with an apple and leave them at room temperature for one or two days.) Or you can make the mousse in one large mold and serve as hors d'oeuvres, again surrounded by sliced fresh pears. Guests help themselves with a knife. If you leave out the gelatin, you will have a perfectly delicious creamy Roquefort dressing.

6	egg yolks
6	tablespoons heavy cream
1	package unflavored gelatin, dissolved in
¼	cup water
¾	pound Roquefort cheese
1½	cups heavy cream
3	egg whites, beaten stiff
	Fresh pears, sliced

In a heavy saucepan, beat the egg yolks and 6 tablespoons heavy cream over low heat until light and creamy, making sure not to curdle the mixture. Add dissolved gelatin, mix well and remove from heat. Force the Roquefort cheese through a sieve or strainer, add it to the egg-yolk mixture and cool. Whip the heavy cream until stiff and fold into mixture. Then fold in beaten egg whites. Pour into lightly oiled molds and refrigerate for at least 2 hours.

Unmold and serve surrounded by sliced fresh pears.

Yield: 16 servings as hors d'oeuvres

Cheese and Chutney Puffs

This recipe is not only wonderful for hors d'oeuvres, but it also makes a great lunch when put on regular-size slices of white bread. Line your cookie sheet with aluminum foil. It helps with the cleanup.

1	loaf thin-sliced white bread, cut into 1-inch rounds
2	cups grated Cheddar cheese
1	egg
½	cup bread crumbs
2	tablespoons chili sauce
2	dashes Tabasco
	Chutney

Put the toast rounds into a 350°F. oven for about 5 minutes to dry them. Mix the cheese, egg, bread crumbs, chili sauce and Tabasco, combining the ingredients well; then make small, round balls, put each on a toast round and make a depression in the middle. Put a small piece of chutney as well as a little of the chutney liquid in each hole. Bake in a preheated 450°F. oven for about 10 minutes.

Yield: approximately 32 puffs

Crêpes Filled with Spinach and Mushrooms

In case you have a friend who is a vegetarian, this recipe is wonderful as you can serve these to the rest of the guests as well. By the way, the beer gives the crêpes a wonderful flavor, but you may substitute ½ cup milk for the beer, if you prefer.

Crêpes:

½	cup milk
½	cup beer
3	eggs
1	cup all-purpose flour
3	tablespoons butter, melted
1	tablespoon butter for cooking crêpes

Put all ingredients except butter for cooking crêpes in blender, blend well, let batter rest for at least 30 minutes. In a crêpe pan or small skillet (preferably Teflon type), melt a little butter over medium heat. When the pan is very hot, wipe excess butter from it with a paper towel. Pour in enough batter to just cover the bottom of the pan. When crêpe is lightly browned around the edges, turn it quickly with a small metal spatula and cook it for another 2 seconds. Turn out onto a piece of waxed paper or foil, cover with another piece of paper or foil and continue until you have 12 crêpes.

Sauce:

4	tablespoons butter
6	tablespoons all-purpose flour
2½	cups milk
½	cup heavy cream
	Salt and pepper to taste
1	teaspoon lemon juice
1	cup grated Parmesan cheese

Melt the butter in a saucepan, add flour and stir with a whisk until smooth. Add 2 cups milk, whisk until smooth and simmer 2 to 3 minutes. Pour off ¾ cup of this white sauce into a mixing bowl (to be used later for the filling), then add the other ½ cup milk and the heavy cream to the saucepan. Season with salt and pepper, add the lemon juice and Parmesan cheese and beat until smooth. Put aside.

Filling:

2	tablespoons butter
2	tablespoons chopped scallions
1	pound fresh mushrooms, cleaned and sliced
1	pound frozen chopped spinach, thawed

Melt the butter in a sautéing pan, add the scallions and mushrooms and sauté 4 minutes. Then add the spinach, lemon juice, and salt and pepper. Combine well and sauté 2 minutes more. Add the ¾ cup sauce; remove from heat. Fill each crêpe with this mixture and roll them up.

Preheat oven to 375°F. Pour one-quarter of the sauce from the saucepan into an ovenproof dish. Place crêpes on top. Pour the rest of the sauce over them and heat in the oven about 10 minutes or until sauce begins to bubble. Then place under broiler until the top is golden brown. Serve immediately.

½ teaspoon lemon juice

Salt and pepper to taste

¾ cup white sauce

Everything in this dish can be made in advance and refrigerated: the crêpes, the sauce, the filling. But save the assembly to the last minute because otherwise the crêpes will get soggy.

Yield: 12 servings as first course or 6 servings as luncheon

Dilled Crêpes with Smoked Salmon

Crêpes are definitely one of the most versatile dishes around, and you can serve them for a very elegant breakfast or brunch as well as for luncheon. Or how about as a first course or an after-theater supper? This dish would be appropriate and appreciated, I am sure, on any of these occasions.

Crêpes:

½ cup milk

½ cup beer

3 eggs

1 cup all-purpose flour

3 tablespoons butter, melted

2 tablespoons chopped dill

1 tablespoon butter for cooking crêpes

Put all ingredients except butter for cooking crêpes in blender, blend well, let batter rest for at least 30 minutes. In a crêpe pan or small skillet (preferably Teflon type), melt a little butter over medium heat. When the pan is very hot, wipe excess butter from it with a paper towel. Pour in enough batter to just cover the bottom of the pan. When crêpe is lightly browned around the edges, turn it quickly with a small metal spatula and cook it for another 2 seconds. Turn out onto a piece of waxed paper or foil, cover with another piece of paper or foil and continue.

Yield: 12 crêpes

Filling:

1 slice smoked salmon per crêpe, sliced paper thin

3 tablespoons scallions, very finely chopped

3 tablespoons capers, very finely chopped

1 cup sour cream

Fresh dill sprigs

Fill each crêpe with a slice of smoked salmon, sprinkle with scallions and capers and fold. Decorate a serving platter with some lettuce leaves; arrange the crêpes on it in a row. Put a tablespoon of sour cream and a sprig of fresh dill on each crêpe. Garnish the platter if you wish with lemon slices and fresh dill or parsley.

Yield: 12 servings as first course or 6 servings as luncheon

Crêpes Farci

This is a great dish for an after-theater supper, lunch or elegant first course. You can make it all ahead of time except for filling the crêpes, which get too soggy if they sit too long after they are filled.

Crêpes:

½ cup milk

½ cup beer

3 eggs

1 cup all-purpose flour

3 tablespoons butter, melted

1 tablespoon butter for cooking crêpes

Put all ingredients except butter for cooking crêpes in a blender and blend well. Let batter rest for at least 30 minutes. Take a crêpe pan or small skillet and put a little butter in it. When very hot, wipe the pan with a paper towel so all excess fat is gone. Pour some of the batter in the pan, making sure there is just enough to cover the bottom. Leave the crêpe until it gets lightly brown on the edges, then turn over and cook a couple of seconds longer. Place crêpe on a piece of waxed paper or foil, cover with another piece of paper or foil. Continue until you have made 12 crêpes.

Cream Sauce:

4 tablespoons butter

6 tablespoons all-purpose flour

2½ cups milk

½ cup heavy cream

Salt and pepper to taste

1 teaspoon lemon juice

Melt the butter in a saucepan, add flour and stir until smooth. Pour in 2 cups milk at once, whisk until smooth and simmer for 2 or 3 minutes. Pour ¾ cup of the sauce into a mixing bowl (to be used later for the shrimp filling), then pour the remaining ½ cup milk and the cream into the sauce in the saucepan. Add salt and pepper and the lemon juice and whisk until smooth.

Filling:

1 pound shrimp

2 tablespoons butter

2 tablespoons scallions, chopped

¾ cup cream sauce

1 tablespoon dill, chopped

½ teaspoon lemon juice

Salt and pepper to taste

Preheat oven to 375°F. Shell and devein the shrimp and cut about ¼ inch thick. Melt butter in a saucepan, add scallions, sauté for 1 minute. Add shrimp and sauté until pink. Add the ¾ cup sauce you put aside, dill, lemon juice, salt and pepper, and mix together.

Fill each crêpe and roll up. Pour about ¼ cup of sauce into an ovenproof dish, put crêpes on top of it, coat the crêpes with the rest of the sauce.

Topping:

1 *tablespoon bread crumbs*

1 *tablespoon Switzerland Swiss cheese, grated*

1 *tablespoon butter*

Mix bread crumbs, cheese and butter together. Scatter the topping over crêpes. Put in oven for 10 minutes, or until golden brown.

Yield: 12 servings as first course or 6 servings as luncheon

Soufflés

If I were to name the dishes that most intimidate people in cooking, soufflés would have to be at the top of the list. Well, once you understand the basics, the why and how, of soufflés, you will find yourself turning them out in all flavors and shapes without batting an eyelash.

Soufflés come in two categories: sweet and savory; the basic principle is the same in both. A hot soufflé is structured into three parts.

The Basic Sauce: A combination of butter, flour and liquid.

The Flavoring: In sweet soufflés, this can be liqueurs, pureed fruits, chocolate, etc. In savory soufflés, cheese; concentrated stock; pureed or finely chopped vegetables, meats or fish; and egg yolks.

The Egg Whites: These are what will make your soufflés rise. Make sure egg whites are beaten until stiff, incorporating as much air as possible either by hand, with a whisk, or with a good electric mixer. Don't overbeat to dry stage or you will not be able to fold them into your sauce.

Important Pointers.

1. Make sure your oven is preheated to anywhere from 350° to 400°F. The larger the soufflé dish, the lower the heat. The smaller, the higher the heat.
2. Make sure there are no lumps in the sauce. This can be avoided by using a whisk. Your sauce should be rather firm, otherwise your soufflé will collapse too easily.
3. When using liqueurs, use the best quality; in fruits, the ripest; in chocolate you can use bittersweet, semisweet or sweet, depending upon what you prefer.
4. Cheeses should be strong-flavored ones, such as Cheddar, Parmesan, etc. Stocks should be double strength to give flavor. It is important that whatever nonliquid flavoring you use be either finely chopped or pureed. If not, your soufflé will not rise properly.
5. Before adding the egg yolks, turn off heat, as they might otherwise curdle.
6. If beating egg whites by hand, have them at room temperature. They will whip more easily, and you can incorporate more air. When making a sweet soufflé, add about 3 tablespoons of sugar to your egg whites once they start to get stiff. This will give them more body.
7. When folding the beaten egg whites into your sauce, do so gently. The more you mix, the more air you lose.
8. Always butter your soufflé dish. You will get a better crust, and the dish will be easier to clean.

9. You can keep the soufflé in a pan of hot water for up to 1 hour before baking. Make sure the water does not boil.
10. Once soufflés are baked they must be served and eaten immediately.
11. Soufflés should always be slightly runny in the middle.

Problems.

Soufflé Does Not Rise:

1. You did not beat your egg whites properly.
2. You mixed too much when you folded your sauce into the egg whites, removing too much air.
3. Your oven temperature was too low.
4. Your sauce was too thick, or a flavoring ingredient was not chopped or pureed finely enough.

Soufflé Collapses:

1. Your sauce was not thick enough.
2. You baked soufflé too long.
3. A sudden draft or high temperature change occurred.

Cheese Soufflé

I have this recipe in my first cookbook. The only change I have made here is to use a different amount of cheese to make it a little lighter, but this is still one of my most favorite and popular soufflés. Instead of Cheddar cheese, you may use ½ cup freshly grated Parmesan cheese and ½ cup grated Switzerland cheese, which will then make it a Mornay Soufflé.

4	tablespoons butter
4	tablespoons all-purpose flour
1½	cups milk
1½	cups grated sharp Cheddar cheese
	Pinch of nutmeg
	Salt and pepper to taste
6	eggs, separated

Melt the butter in a heavy saucepan. Stir in the flour and blend well. Add the milk, stirring constantly with a whisk until it comes to a boil. Add the cheese and stir until it melts. Add the nutmeg and salt and pepper. Take pan off heat. Add the egg yolks one by one, stirring well after each. Beat the egg whites until stiff and fold them carefully into the cheese sauce. Pour into a buttered 2-quart soufflé dish. Bake in a 375°F. oven for about 30 minutes.

Yield: 8 servings as first course or 4 to 6 servings as luncheon

Soufflé Florentine

This makes a most unusual first course or, if you like, a luncheon dish. It is very easy to make and looks spectacular. I definitely suggest that you use glass soufflé dishes since the two-layer effect of the spinach and cheese looks very pretty. The only step to watch out for is to remember to poach your eggs in advance, keeping them cold in the refrigerator, since you don't want them to cook anymore when you bake the soufflé.

4	tablespoons butter
4	tablespoons all-purpose flour
1½	cups milk
	Salt and pepper to taste
1	package frozen chopped spinach, thawed
6	eggs, separated
	Nutmeg
¼	cup grated Switzerland Swiss cheese
½	cup grated Parmesan cheese
8	eggs, poached and kept in the refrigerator

Melt the butter in a heavy saucepan. Add the flour and combine well. Cook for a few minutes without letting it brown, then add the milk, stirring constantly with a whisk until sauce comes to a boil. Simmer for 2 minutes and season with salt and pepper. Add the spinach to one-half the sauce, bring to a boil, and simmer for 2 minutes, stirring constantly. Then add 3 egg yolks and a little nutmeg. Add the cheeses to the other half of the sauce and combine until melted. Add 3 egg yolks and combine well. Beat egg whites until stiff, divide them in half and fold gently into the sauces.

Take 8 individual soufflé dishes, butter them, then put some of the spinach mixture in the bottom of each. Gently place a poached egg on top of the spinach, and cover it with the cheese mixture. Put in a preheated 400°F. oven for about 10 to 15 minutes. Serve immediately.

Yield: 8 servings

Omelettes

Making omelettes, like making hot soufflés, seems to really intimidate most cooks. This is pure nonsense. Particularly with the advent of the Teflon-type pan, anybody can make a beautiful omelette. There are just two simple methods: the savory omelette is made from whole eggs and the soufflé omelette is made from whole eggs separated. (Basic Savory Omelette recipe follows. See page 144 for a basic soufflé omelette.)

Once you have made the basic omelette, it can be filled with anything under the sun and usually is.

Essential: one 6-inch or 8-inch skillet or omelette pan with a Teflon, T-Fal or other nonstick surface. Use this pan for nothing but omelettes and eggs so it doesn't get scratched.

Basic Savory Omelette

2 *eggs*

1 *tablespoon water*

   Dash of Tabasco

   Salt and pepper to taste

1 *tablespoon butter*

Mix the eggs, water, Tabasco, salt and pepper lightly with a fork. Melt the butter in an omelette pan and cook until slightly brown. Pour in the eggs and stir briskly with a fork, pulling the edges of the egg mass toward the center as it thickens. Repeat this until there is no more liquid but the eggs are still very soft. If you want to fill the omelette, put the filling in now. Slide out half of the omelette onto a heated plate. Then lift up the handle of your pan and fold the other half of the omelette over the first.

Omelette Fillings

Salmon:

1 *can salmon, skin and bones removed*

2 *tablespoons fresh lemon juice*

4 *scallions, finely chopped*

2 *dashes Tabasco*

   Salt and pepper to taste

Combine all ingredients well and let marinate for about 20 minutes. Put about 3 tablespoons of filling on each omelette before folding it.

Yield: filling for 2 to 4 omelettes

Mushroom:

2   tablespoons butter

2   tablespoons chopped
    shallots

½   pound fresh
    mushrooms, cleaned
    and sliced

    Salt and pepper to
    taste

2   tablespoons chopped
    parsley

Melt the butter in a heavy sautéing pan, add the shallots and sauté them for about 2 minutes. Then add the mushrooms and continue sautéing for another 2 minutes. Season with salt and pepper and add the parsley; combine well and put about 3 tablespoons of filling on each omelette before folding it.

Yield: filling for 2 to 4 omelettes

Other Fillings.

Cheddar Cheese: ½ cup grated sharp Cheddar cheese for each omelette. Sprinkle the Cheddar cheese on the omelette just before it sets. Continue cooking the omelette until done, fold and serve.

Parmesan or Switzerland Swiss cheese: ½ cup of either, or any combination of both amounting to ½ cup for each omelette. Proceed as in Cheddar cheese omelette.

Chopped scallions, or a mixture of *chopped fresh herbs,* such as parsley, tarragon and dill, or whatever else is available.

Tomato Fondue: Recipe in vegetable section. Add some fresh chopped basil to it.

Leftover ham, finely cut

Leftover chicken, finely cut

Leftover turkey, finely cut

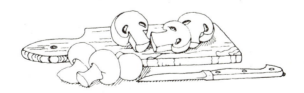

All About Stocks

A stock is the essence, or flavor if you like, of meat, fowl or fish that has been fortified by the addition of vegetables, herbs, wine, etc. The key, however, lies in the essence itself because it provides most of the flavor. It must be strong!

Most enthusiasts, once they decide to take cooking seriously, feel compelled to make their own stocks. The necessity of this is generally emphasized by most classic French cookbooks. Believe me, in most cases it is a myth, and a very frustrating one at that.

It is possible, for example, to extract the essence from beef if you have a lot of beef and a lot of time. But you will find that attempting it will usually provide you with a liquid that doesn't taste all that great. Remember, a restaurant chef has an unending supply of meat and bones to add to his stockpot and someone to watch and skim it. Unless you operate a big restaurant, I suggest that you leave this laborious task to people better equipped to do the job and save your creative energy and money for things that are more fun. This does not mean that I do not make or use homemade stocks. It simply means I reserve doing it for when it is really necessary. For instance, in the case of fish stock, there aren't any good commercial ones available, or I may have a lot of chicken backs and wings in my freezer and want to use them up, or I may want to make chicken noodle soup. If your butcher bones a rib of veal for you, or you buy a whole shoulder as I often do, by all means have the butcher cut the bones into smaller pieces—you are paying for them anyhow—and you can make veal stock. Buying the veal bones separately, though, is a very expensive proposition.

Here are the recipes for making a good stock when you do decide to make one and some tips that apply to all homemade stocks:

1. Once you remove the scum, after the stock comes to a boil, simply add several eggshells (which you saved from breakfast); this will save you the bother of further skimming, since the scum adheres to the eggshells.
2. Be careful not to add too many carrots. Stick with just one, since they have a tendency to make your stock too sweet.
3. Do not add too much salt in the beginning. You might decide to reduce the stock later and it could become oversalted.
4. After the stock has been strained, it is easier to remove the fat if you refrigerate your stock until cold; the fat will rise and harden. Of course, this does not apply when you need the stock immediately.
5. Whenever I make a large quantity, I freeze it in 16-ounce plastic containers, since most recipes call for 1 to 2 cups.
6. In the case of veal stock, I reduce it until it is quite strong, cool it, remove the fat and then freeze the stock in ice-cube trays. When it is solidly frozen, I put the cubes into a plastic bag. They will help me make an almost instant fabulous sauce for my veal scaloppine.

Chicken Stock

6   pounds chicken backs, wings, skin, etc., that you save in your freezer

1   carrot, coarsely chopped

2   stalks celery, coarsely chopped

1   onion, peeled and cut into quarters

1   leek, coarsely chopped

    Bouquet garni (1 bay leaf, 3 sprigs parsley, 1 celery leaf tied together with a cotton string)

6   peppercorns

1   teaspoon salt

    Enough water to cover the ingredients by 1 full inch

Put all the ingredients into a large stockpot and bring to a boil. Remove the scum that rises to the surface, reduce the heat to the lowest level and simmer your stock for approximately 3 hours. Remove the meat and bones from the stock, strain it, skim off the fat, cool. The stock will keep for at least one week in the refrigerator. If you would like to have a more concentrated stock, simply return the strained stock to a clean saucepan and continue simmering to reduce it to the strength you wish.

Yield: approximately 3 quarts stock

White Veal Stock

5   pounds veal bones

3   pounds veal shins or trimmings of veal

1   carrot, coarsely chopped

2   stalks celery, coarsely chopped

1   onion, peeled and cut into quarters

1   leek, coarsely chopped

    Bouquet garni (1 bay leaf, 3 sprigs parsley, 1 celery leaf, tied together with a cotton string)

6   peppercorns

1   teaspoon salt

    Enough water to cover the ingredients by 1 full inch

Put all the ingredients into a large stockpot and bring to a boil. Remove the scum that rises to the surface. Reduce the heat to the lowest level and simmer your stock for approximately 5 hours. Remove the meat and bones from the stock, strain it and skim off the fat. If not for immediate use, cool the stock and put it into containers. Freeze it or store in the refrigerator, where it will keep for at least one week. If you would like to have a more concentrated stock, simply return the strained stock to a clean saucepan and continue simmering to reduce it to the strength you wish.

Yield: approximately 3 quarts stock

Brown Veal Stock

Use the same ingredients as for White Veal Stock, but brown your meat, bones and vegetables in a little vegetable oil in a sautéing pan or in the oven. (I prefer the sautéing pan, since it goes faster and uses less energy.)

Fish Stock

2   pounds fish bones and heads (Your fish market will be happy to supply these for you; halibut and flounder are fine.)

1   onion, stuck with a clove

1   stalk celery, chopped

1   carrot, chopped

1   leek, chopped

Bouquet garni (1 bay leaf, 3 sprigs parsley, 1 celery leaf, tied together with a cotton string)

3   cups dry white wine

2   cups water

6   peppercorns

1   teaspoon salt

Shells of 3 eggs (to absorb the surface scum)

Combine all ingredients in a heavy saucepan and bring to a boil. Lower heat and simmer for 40 minutes. Strain.

Yield: approximately 2 quarts stock

Note: Make sure not to use bones from fish such as blue fish or mackerel as their flavor is too strong.

Shrimp Stock

Next time your recipe calls for raw shrimp, which you have to clean, take the shells and put them into a saucepan. Cover them with water and a little dry white wine, some parsley or fresh dill, bring to a boil, and simmer for about 20 minutes. You can use this stock in sauces that go with shrimp, or it will do if you don't have fish stock.

Soups

The flavors, varieties and uses of soup are virtually limitless. Whether served as a first course or main dish, soup is always a winner. In fact, one of my more successful parties was a soup party. It was on the occasion of the publishing of my second cookbook, and everybody seemed by far to prefer soup to the usual cocktail food. Ever since, I have made soup for my Christmas open-house party.

Wonderful canned chicken and beef broth are now produced. My personal favorites most of the time are the double-strength brands, as I can do many more things with them. Their one drawback is they are generally very salty, so keep that in mind before salting your soup.

Chicken Noodle Soup

This is my daughter's favorite soup. Whenever she comes home from college, she hopes that I have a large pot of it in the refrigerator. Sometimes I do.

Chicken stock made from saved backs and wings, enough to cover

1 chicken, about 3½ pounds

1 bay leaf

4 carrots, peeled and chopped

4 stalks celery, chopped

1 pound green peas

2 zucchini, cut into cubes

2 red peppers, cut into cubes

Very fine soup noodles, cooked in water and rinsed off

Salt and pepper to taste

Chopped fresh parsley, optional

In a large pot, bring the stock to a boil. (Have enough stock to cover the chicken by 3 inches.) Add the chicken and bay leaf. When stock boils again, turn down the heat and gently simmer chicken for 45 minutes, then remove. Discard bay leaf. At this stage, add carrots and celery to soup. Allow to simmer while you remove the skin and bones from the chicken. Cut the chicken into bite-size pieces and return to the soup. Then add peas, zucchini and red peppers and simmer for an additional 2 minutes. Then add the cooked noodles. (The amount of noodles depends on how many you want. I want lots.) Check seasoning and add salt and pepper to taste. I like to top the soup with some chopped fresh parsley. As you can see, this requires quite a bit of work.

Yield: 6 to 8 servings

Zucchini Soup

One of the great joys of summer is the profusion of zucchini. I love it stir-fried, deep-fried, baked, sautéed, and it even makes a great soup. You can improvise on this recipe by adding curry powder instead of thyme. Or you can add cold heavy cream to the soup just before serving.

3 tablespoons butter

2 medium-size onions, sliced

1 teaspoon thyme

4 cups sliced zucchini

4 cups sliced yellow squash

2 10½-ounce cans chicken broth, double strength

2 cans water

Salt and pepper to taste

Heat the butter in the saucepan without letting it brown, then add the onions and sauté them for a few minutes without browning them. Add the thyme, zucchini and squash, and combine well. Then add the chicken broth and water, bring to a boil and simmer for 20 minutes. Season with salt and pepper. Cool the soup and put through a blender. Serve hot or cold and garnish with a thin slice of zucchini or with chopped parsley.

Yield: 4 to 6 servings

Iced Cucumber Soup

If ever there was a cool and elegant soup, this one is it. I sometimes take it along for a picnic lunch, in a Thermos bottle to keep it cold.

3 cucumbers

2 tablespoons vegetable oil

1 onion, chopped

1 10½-ounce can chicken broth, double strength

1 can water

3 tablespoons dill

Salt and pepper to taste

½ cup heavy cream

Peel the cucumbers, cut them in half lengthwise and remove the seeds with a small spoon. Cut the cucumbers into ½-inch-thick slices.

In a heavy saucepan, heat the oil over low heat, then add the onion and sauté for a few minutes without letting it brown. Then add the cucumbers, chicken broth, water, dill, and salt and pepper. Bring to a boil and simmer for 10 minutes. Cool the soup and put through a blender. Blend for 30 seconds, making sure not to fill the blender more than half full. Add the cream and put soup in the refrigerator till serving time. Top each bowl of soup with a sprinkle of fresh dill.

Yield: 4 to 6 servings

Potage Cressonnière

This is a great soup served either hot or cold. Not only does it look great, but it also has a wonderful unusual taste. Believe me, it will turn into one of your favorites.

2 tablespoons butter

2 leeks, cleaned and chopped

3 medium-size potatoes, peeled and sliced

2 10½-ounce cans chicken broth, double strength and

2 cans water or

5 cups homemade stock (instead of canned broth and water)

1 bunch watercress
Salt and pepper to taste

1 cup heavy cream
Watercress leaves

Heat the butter in a saucepan without letting it brown, then add the leeks and sauté them for a few minutes without browning. Add potatoes, chicken broth and water. Bring to a boil and simmer for 20 minutes. Add watercress and salt and pepper and combine well. Cool the soup and put through a blender. Add the cream. Reheat soup gently before serving, or refrigerate and serve cold. Garnish with watercress leaves.

Yield: 4 to 6 servings

Goulash Soup

On a cold night in Germany, you would enjoy this soup in a restaurant after the opera or the theater, or for a hearty lunch. It was never spicy enough for me, so I add cayenne pepper (carefully!). You can also add chopped red and green peppers. Just sauté them with the onions. To make a real Hungarian goulash, just increase the meat in this recipe to 3 pounds. You can also use pork, lamb or veal cubes.

2	tablespoons vegetable oil
4	medium-size yellow onions, chopped
1	pound lean beef (top round), cut into small cubes
	Salt and pepper to taste
¼	teaspoon cumin seed
2	tablespoons paprika
	Pinch of cayenne pepper
2	10½-ounce cans beef broth, double strength
2	cans water
2	medium-size potatoes, peeled and cut into small cubes

In a heavy saucepan, heat the vegetable oil, add the onions and sauté them until they are lightly browned; then add the beef, which you seasoned with salt and pepper. Continue sautéing until beef has browned. Then add the cumin seed and paprika and cayenne and combine well. Add the beef broth and water, bring to a boil, and simmer on low heat for about 1 hour. Add the potatoes and continue simmering until they are done (about 15 minutes).

Yield: 4 to 6 servings

Green Bean Soup

This was the traditional Saturday lunch for one German family where I was apprentice at the age of sixteen, and it is still one of my favorites for a cold winter day. You can also serve it as a vegetable casserole by reducing the liquid to just 1 can of chicken broth and thickening the sauce with a little flour or cornstarch.

We have an herb in Germany called "Bohnenkraut" that is very similar to summer savory but a bit more pungent. When you buy green beans at a German farmers' market, they give you Bohnenkraut to go with the beans. It gives them a great flavor.

4 *slices bacon, chopped*

2 *onions, chopped*

1 *tablespoon summer savory*

1 *pound green beans, washed, ends cut off and cut in half*

2 *10½-ounce cans chicken broth, double strength*

2 *cans water*

2 *tablespoons cider vinegar (approximately)*

Salt and pepper to taste

Chopped fresh parsley (optional)

Cook the bacon in a heavy saucepan. When lightly browned, add the chopped onions. Sauté for another 3 minutes, stirring occasionally, then add the summer savory, green beans, chicken broth, water, vinegar and salt and pepper. Bring to a boil and simmer for another 15 minutes. Serve with some chopped parsley on top.

Yield: 4 to 6 servings

Lentil Soup with Sausages

Here is another German favorite. It makes a great cold-weather lunch or dinner, and if you ski in the winter it's just what you need to come home to.

When you use lentils, or any dried bean, put them in a colander, rinse in cold water and inspect them. Sometimes tiny stones or other impurities get mixed in. And no matter what the package says, always soak them overnight. Always save ham bones and freeze them tightly wrapped for occasions like this. They make a delightful addition to this soup. This recipe can also be used to make a great pea soup. Substitute split peas for the lentils and omit the vinegar.

4 slices bacon, chopped

2 onions, chopped

2 carrots, chopped

2 stalks celery, chopped

1 pound lentils, soaked overnight and drained

3 10½-ounce cans chicken broth, double strength

3 cans water

1 bay leaf

4 smoked sausages, sliced

Salt and pepper to taste

2 tablespoons vinegar

Put the bacon in a saucepan and cook until it starts to brown. Then add the onions, carrots and celery, and sauté until these vegetables turn light brown. Then add the lentils, chicken broth, water and bay leaf. Bring to a boil and simmer on low heat for about 1 hour. Then add the sausages, season with salt and pepper, and add the vinegar. Taste again and add more if you like.

Yield: 6 to 8 servings

Black Mushroom Soup

1 pound mushrooms, sliced

2 10½-ounce cans beef broth, double strength

2 cans water

1 ounce cognac

Salt and pepper to taste

Combine all ingredients in a saucepan and bring to a boil. Simmer for 40 minutes. Then strain the mushrooms out and serve the consommé in cups.

Yield: 4 to 6 servings

Butternut Squash and Apple Soup

1   *small butternut squash (about 1 pound)*

3   *tart green apples*

1   *medium onion*

¼   *teaspoon rosemary*

¼   *teaspoon marjoram*

3   *10½-ounce cans chicken broth, double strength*

2   *cans water*

2   *slices white bread*

    Salt and pepper to taste

¼   *cup heavy cream*

1   *tablespoon parsley, freshly chopped*

Cut the butternut squash in half, peel and seed. Peel, core and coarsely chop the apples. Peel the onion and also chop coarsely. Combine all these ingredients with the rosemary, marjoram, chicken broth, water, bread, salt and pepper in a heavy saucepan. Bring to a boil and simmer uncovered for 45 minutes.

Puree the soup in a blender until smooth. Do in several batches, not filling the blender more than a quarter full each time. Return the soup to the saucepan and bring to a boil, then reduce heat. Just before serving, add the heavy cream. Serve hot with a sprinkle of freshly chopped parsley on top.

Yield: 6 to 8 servings

Crème Olga

4   *tablespoons butter*

5   *bunches scallions, finely chopped*

    Salt and pepper to taste

2   *10½-ounce cans chicken broth, double strength*

2   *cans water*

¾   *pound fresh mushrooms, sliced*

1   *cup light cream*

Melt the butter in a heavy saucepan, add the scallions and sauté for ten minutes. Season with salt and pepper, add chicken broth and water and simmer for 15 minutes.

Then add the mushrooms, bring to a boil and turn off the heat. Cool the soup and put through a blender. Pour back in saucepan, add cream, reheat and serve.

Yield: 4 to 6 servings

Main Courses

Lamb

American lamb is the finest in the world and is definitely my favorite red meat. According to the Lamb Council, the term "spring lamb" applies to lamb five to eight months old. Younger than that, it is called "baby lamb" and older than one year, it is called "mutton." You can generally tell the age of lamb by the color of the fat—the whiter it is, the younger the lamb. All of my recipes are for spring lamb, which is available year round.

When cooking lamb, I always remove all of the fat as well as the fell, which is the thin membrane surrounding the meat. For flavoring lamb, I think garlic, lemon juice, rosemary and thyme are superb. But always keep in mind that you want to perfume the meat, not overpower it. Inserting garlic cloves, for example, in a leg of lamb concentrates the flavor too much in one area. And, if not removed, a clove will end up in a bite of lamb, thus creating a garlic-hater.

Much has been said, and much should be said, about the custom of cooking a leg of lamb until it is gray and dried out. The only people this is good for are the mint-jelly makers. I have served pink lamb to many people who not only adore it but also don't know what it is. They usually mistake it for beef.

Rack of Lamb Persille

This is a most elegant dish. I prepared it many times for Mrs. Kennedy and her guests. It can also be made as a "saddle of lamb" when the butcher leaves the racks from both sides connected.

In the days of my apprenticeship, we used to serve a "baron of lamb," which is the saddle, as well as the hindquarters. What a glorious sight that was. I always felt sorry for the butler, who had to carry it to the dining room, as it certainly is heavier than a rack of lamb.

When ordering a rack of lamb, make sure the butcher cracks the bones on the bottom. Otherwise it is very difficult to carve. Covering the exposed bones with aluminum foil during cooking will prevent burning.

2 tablespoons vegetable oil

2 carrots, cut into pieces

2 stalks celery, cut into pieces

1 large onion, coarsely chopped

1 teaspoon thyme

½ cup beef broth, double strength

½ cup chicken broth, double strength

½ cup dry white wine

2 racks of lamb, each weighing about 2½ pounds

Juice of 1 lemon

1 clove garlic, put through garlic press

2 teaspoons thyme

Salt and pepper to taste

1 cup bread crumbs

3 tablespoons butter, melted

1 clove garlic, put through garlic press

½ cup parsley, finely chopped

Salt and pepper to taste

Preheat oven to 400°F. Heat the oil in a heavy sautéing pan and add the carrots, celery, onion and 1 teaspoon thyme. Sauté until lightly browned, then add the beef broth, chicken broth and white wine. Bring to a boil, reduce heat and simmer.

Rub the lamb well with lemon juice, 1 clove garlic, 2 teaspoons thyme, salt and pepper. Put a metal rack into your roasting pan and place the lamb on top. Pour the sauce and vegetables into the pan, and roast lamb for 25 minutes. Baste several times during that period. After 25 minutes, remove the pan from the oven and raise the temperature to 500°F.

Mix together the bread crumbs, melted butter, 1 clove garlic, parsley, salt and pepper. Press the bread-crumb-and-parsley mixture onto the top of the racks and return to the oven for 5 minutes or until golden brown. Remove from the oven and transfer the lamb to a preheated serving platter. Strain the sauce and serve on the side.

Yield: 4 to 6 servings

Rack of Baby Lamb

When I did a Cookingschool in Omaha, Nebraska, I met the kind of butcher every cook dreams about. He knew how to buy meat, to cut it and to portion it. He had a display of the most luscious little racks of baby lamb I have ever seen. I couldn't resist bringing some back to New York and creating this recipe.

1   *rack of baby lamb*

     Juice of 1 lemon

1   *clove garlic, put through garlic press*

1   *teaspoon rosemary*

3   *tablespoons vegetable oil*

     Salt and pepper to taste

2   *carrots, peeled and cut into julienne strips*

2   *stalks celery, peeled and cut into julienne strips*

2   *leeks, washed and cut into julienne strips*

½   *cup dry white wine*

½   *cup chicken broth, double strength*

1   *teaspoon beef extract (Bovril)*

Rub the lamb with the lemon juice, garlic and rosemary, and marinate at room temperature for about 20 minutes. In a heavy sautéing pan, heat the oil, then season the lamb with salt and pepper and brown it on all sides in the oil. Remove lamb and add the carrots, celery and leeks to the pan; sauté them for about 2 minutes. Add the wine, chicken broth and beef extract, and bring to a boil. Place the rack of lamb on top of the vegetables, cover, lower the heat and simmer for 15 to 20 minutes, basting occasionally.

Serve lamb on the bed of vegetables. You may thicken the sauce, if you like, with a little cornstarch mixed in cold water.

Yield: 2 to 4 servings

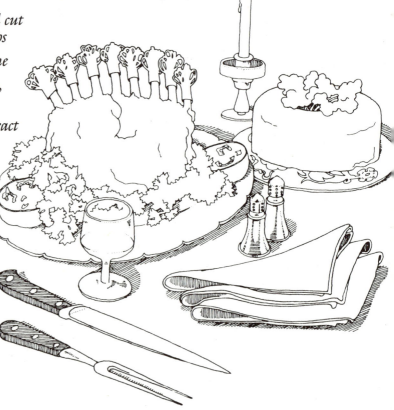

Lamb Casserole

This is a hearty dish that should be served with a crisp salad and some hot, crusty French bread on a cold day. It can be completely cooked several days in advance. It also freezes well. You may substitute shoulder chops for the leg of lamb in which case you reduce the cooking time to about 45 minutes, depending on their thickness.

3 tablespoons vegetable oil

3 pounds lean lamb (from the leg), cut into 1-inch pieces

2 onions, chopped

2 cloves garlic, put through garlic press

2 tablespoons summer savory

1 teaspoon thyme

1 tablespoon tomato paste

1 can tomatoes (2-pound)

1 10½-ounce can beef broth, double strength

1 can water

  Salt and pepper to taste

2 red peppers, cleaned and coarsely chopped

2 green peppers, cleaned and coarsely chopped

1 pound fresh green beans, cut into 1-inch lengths

  Freshly chopped parsley

Heat the oil in a heavy sautéing pan, then add the lamb and brown it. (Make sure the pieces do not touch each other.) Remove the lamb and put aside; then add the onions and garlic to the pan and sauté until lightly browned. Return the lamb to the pan and add the summer savory, thyme, tomato paste, tomatoes, beef broth, water, salt and pepper. Bring to a boil and simmer covered for 1 hour, then add the peppers and green beans, and simmer for another 30 minutes.

Serve with some freshly chopped parsley on top.

Yield: 6 servings

Stuffed Leg of Lamb

Whenever I cook a leg of lamb, I always ask the butcher to bone it. It makes carving a lot easier and allows me to stuff it with something that will perfume the whole leg.

1   leg of lamb, boned (about 6 to 7 pounds)

    Juice of 1 lemon

½   cup soy sauce

    Salt and pepper to taste

1   clove garlic, put through garlic press

½   cup finely chopped parsley

½   cup bread crumbs

1   teaspoon rosemary

1   carrot, chopped

1   onion, coarsely chopped

½   teaspoon rosemary

1   10½-ounce can chicken broth, double strength

1   10½-ounce can beef broth, double strength

1   cup dry white wine

Preheat the oven to 400°F. Lay the lamb skin-side down on a flat surface and rub it with lemon juice and soy sauce, then season it with salt and pepper.

Combine the garlic, parsley, bread crumbs and 1 teaspoon rosemary, and mix together well. Spread this mixture over the lamb and into the pockets left by the boning, then roll the meat into a cylindrical shape to enclose the stuffing completely. Tie loops of string around the lamb and put it in a roasting pan.

Surround the lamb with the carrot, onion, celery and ½ teaspoon rosemary, and put in your preheated oven.

Mix the chicken broth, beef broth and wine, and baste the lamb with this liquid after 15 minutes of roasting. Continue basting every 10 minutes for another hour. Before carving, let the lamb rest for 10 minutes outside the oven. In the meantime, put the gravy through a strainer to remove the vegetables. Reheat gravy before serving.

Yield: 8 to 10 servings

Lamb Kabobs

This is a dish that is particularly well suited to barbecue cooking, although it also works well in your broiler. All the preparations are made ahead of time, and at a barbecue your guests can cook their own kabobs to their taste. Just mark handles of the skewers with colored tapes to avoid mix-ups. I suggest serving the kabobs with a big salad and herbed rice. You can substitute pork, veal or skinned and boned chicken breasts for the lamb.

1   boned leg of lamb, well trimmed of fat, and cut into 2-inch cubes

20 white onions, peeled and parboiled for 3 minutes (Peel the onions, which, by the way, are a different variety and smaller than the more common yellow-skinned ones, and cut a shallow cross into each end with your paring knife. This will prevent the onions from pulling apart.)

5   red peppers, cut into wide strips

5   green peppers, cut into wide strips (These, too, may be parboiled if you like. I prefer them very crunchy.)

20 cherry tomatoes

Marinade:

1   cup soy sauce

¼   cup vegetable oil

2   cloves garlic, put through garlic press

1   tablespoon rosemary

1   tablespoon honey

    Juice of 2 lemons

Add the cubed lamb to the Marinade, coat it well and marinate at least 1 hour. If you can marinate it longer, so much the better. Just make sure it is refrigerated and covered with plastic wrap.

Oil long, stainless-steel skewers and fill them, alternating pepper, lamb, tomato, lamb, etc. Cook over medium heat, turning often to brown on all sides—about 15 to 20 minutes.

Yield: 8 servings

Combine all ingredients of the marinade in a bowl and mix well with a fork or whisk.

Polynesian Lamb

If you like to barbecue, this is the recipe for you. It has an almost sweet-and-sour taste. You can marinate the lamb the night before so as to leave you more time with your guests. One butterflied leg of lamb, which is simply a boned leg cut open to be flat, will serve 8 people generously. By the way, your butcher will be delighted to do this for you, saving your energy for something else.

1   leg of lamb, boned and butterflied

Marinade:

1   can frozen pineapple juice

½   cup honey

4   tablespoons soy sauce

1   teaspoon powdered ginger

3   cloves garlic, put through garlic press

¼   cup cider vinegar

¼   cup vegetable oil

Salt and pepper to taste

Put all marinade ingredients into a saucepan, bring to a boil, and simmer for 3 minutes. Place the lamb in a large roasting pan. Pour the marinade over it and coat well on both sides. Marinate at least 1 hour, turning several times. Place lamb on a medium-hot charcoal grill and cook for 5 minutes or until flames have seared one side. Turn, and sear reverse side. Then continue to cook as if it were a sirloin steak, to the desired tenderness. I personally prefer lamb medium rare. Serve the reserved marinade on the side.

Yield: 8 servings

Marinated Lamb with Rosemary

If there was ever a more perfect marriage of flavors than lamb and rosemary, I have not found it. In many fine European restaurants, they broil a whole side of lamb on a spit, continually brushing it with rosemary leaves and marinade. The aroma of the hickory smoke and rosemary is absolutely heavenly.

1	*leg of lamb, boned and butterflied*

Marinade:

	Juice of 1 lemon
¼	*cup soy sauce*
2	*cloves garlic, put through garlic press*
1	*tablespoon dried rosemary*
	Salt and pepper to taste

Combine the marinade ingredients and rub well into the lamb on all sides. Marinate at least 30 minutes. Cook over charcoal or in a broiler for about 20 minutes on each side.

Yield: 8 servings

Note: Whenever you use soy sauce, make sure you use a natural one. A good soy sauce is made from 50 percent soybean and 50 percent wheat, which is carefully selected; then salt is added, as well as genus of yeast, called "Aspergillus sojae." Making soy sauce is fairly involved and not unlike making wine. The whole process, until it is bottled, takes about 6 months. One with a lower salt content is now produced also.

Veal

A few years ago when I first started to do my cooking classes for charity organizations across the country, I realized that it was nearly impossible to find top-quality veal in many parts of the United States, and that furthermore, what was being sold as veal was really young grass-fed beef. This piqued my natural curiosity about all things food, so I decided to investigate.

Following World War II, the United States virtually gave away huge stockpiles of powdered milk, and with it the Dutch manufactured a special formula of milk, vitamins and minerals to feed young calves, to produce what we call milk-fed veal. I toured a plant in New Jersey where they make and package the formula, which is very scientifically changed for each stage of the animals' growth during a sixteen-week period. Then I inspected a veal farm where the animals are raised.

I had heard stories about these animals being force-fed in the dark and generally being mistreated. I am happy to report this is not the case. These bull calves, if they were not being raised for veal, would be slaughtered at birth. The females are raised as dairy cows. The calves are kept in spacious, brightly lit barns, where they are fed the milk formula three times a day. Since they are raised on a diet of milk rather than grass, the color of veal is light pink rather than red.

In today's marketplace, veal is no longer the luxury it used to be. Beef prices have long since passed veal prices, and remember, you have very little fat or waste on veal.

Veal à la Tober

I created this dish for this cookbook, and when finished it's beautiful to look at. Since Guy Tober provided the magnificent loin of veal, I named it for him. Now he can feel as important as the Duke of Wellington.

1	loin of veal, boned
1	tablespoon thyme
	Salt and pepper to taste
4	tablespoons butter
2	tablespoons vegetable oil
½	cup chopped shallots
1	pound fresh mushrooms, sliced
2	cups veal stock or chicken stock
1	cup white wine
1	tablespoon butter mixed with
1	tablespoon cornstarch
½	cup heavy cream
4	medium zucchini, cut into strips

Season the veal with the thyme, salt and pepper, rubbing it in well. In a heavy sautéing pan, heat the 4 tablespoons butter and the oil, add the veal and brown on all sides. Remove veal from pan, add shallots and mushrooms, sauté until lightly browned, then add the stock and white wine. Bring to a boil, return the veal loin to the pan, cover, reduce heat and simmer for about 1 hour. Remove the veal to a carving board.

Thicken the sauce with the cornstarch-butter mixture, then add the heavy cream, making sure not to let the sauce boil. Steam the zucchini for 2 minutes while you slice the veal and put it on a preheated serving platter. Pour some of the sauce over the veal and arrange zucchini around the sides of the platter.

Yield: 6 to 8 servings

Veal Piccata

The most important thing to remember about veal is—don't overcook it. That is particularly true when you are cooking veal scallops or veal cutlets or veal scaloppine; all of these mean the same cut of veal. If you order veal scallops from a butcher who knows his business, he will cut the scallop from the leg and pound it thin with the flat side of a cleaver. Obviously then, it needs very little cooking. Veal Piccata is a very popular and simple dish, basically veal in lemon and butter. In the following recipe for it, you can substitute Marsala wine for the white wine and you have Veal Marsala.

6   veal scallops

     Juice of 1 lemon

1   teaspoon oil

2   tablespoons butter

1   tablespoon all-purpose
     flour

     Salt and pepper to
     taste

¼   cup dry white wine

2   tablespoons finely
     chopped parsley

¼   cup chicken broth,
     double strength

     Beurre manié (1
     teaspoon each of butter
     and flour mixed
     together)

Sprinkle the veal with lemon juice and let stand for a few minutes. Heat the oil and butter in a heavy sautéing pan until very hot. Add the veal, after lightly dusting with flour and seasoning with salt and pepper. Make sure the pieces of veal do not touch each other in the pan. (You might have to cook them in three batches, depending on the size of the pan and veal.) Sauté veal for no more than 1 or 2 minutes on each side.

Remove the veal to a hot serving platter. Add the wine, parsley and chicken broth to the pan juices, and bring to a boil, then add the beurre manié to thicken. Boil for another 2 minutes. Pour the sauce over the veal and serve.

Yield: 6 servings

Veal Birds Orloff

This is an elegant party dish that can be made ahead of time and reheated—gently, please. Count 1 or 2 veal birds per person, depending on the size of the scallops.

If you can make a large amount of veal stock at one time and freeze it in 2-cup containers, the flavor is well worth the effort. Otherwise you can substitute chicken broth.

6	veal scallops
	Lemon juice
	Salt and pepper to taste

Season the veal scallops with lemon juice and salt and pepper. Then put some of the stuffing on one end of each, and roll them up and tie with strings on both ends.

Stuffing:

3	tablespoons butter
3	tablespoons shallots, finely chopped
1	teaspoon thyme
½	cup bread crumbs
2	tablespoons chopped parsley
1	pound ground veal
2	teaspoons cornstarch
1	tablespoon water

To make stuffing, melt the 3 tablespoons butter in a sautéing pan; add the shallots and sauté for a few minutes. Then add the thyme, bread crumbs and parsley and sauté for 1 more minute, combining the ingredients well. Put the ground veal, 2 teaspoons cornstarch and 1 tablespoon water in a bowl and combine them thoroughly, add the sautéed ingredients, mixing well with the veal.

Sauce:

3	tablespoons butter
2	tablespoons vegetable oil
½	pound mushrooms, thinly sliced
1½	cups veal stock
1	tablespoon cornstarch mixed with
1	tablespoon water
½	cup heavy cream

Heat the butter and vegetable oil in a sautéing pan and brown the veal birds on all sides. Then add the mushrooms, continue sautéing for another minute, add the veal stock, bring it to a boil and simmer it on very low heat, covered, for 35 to 40 minutes. Put the veal on a preheated serving platter, thicken the sauce with the cornstarch and water, then add the cream and pour the sauce over your veal. Garnish and serve.

Yield: 6 servings

Veal Cordon Bleu

This is one of the great classic veal dishes and justifiably so. It is easy to prepare and tastes delicious. The important part is to use real Switzerland Swiss cheese and a good boiled ham. The best ham I ever found is called "Prague." It is made by Shaller & Weber, who distribute their products in fine specialty shops all over the country. Above all, do not overcook.

6 large veal scallops

    Fresh lemon juice

    Salt and pepper to taste

6 slices of Switzerland Swiss cheese

6 slices of boiled ham

¼ cup all-purpose flour

2 whole eggs, beaten until well combined

1 cup bread crumbs

4 tablespoons butter

3 tablespoons vegetable oil

Sprinkle the veal with a little lemon juice and let sit for a few minutes. Then season with salt and pepper. Put 1 slice of cheese on half of a veal scallop (if the slice is too big, cut it), and put a slice of ham on top of the cheese, again trimming if too large. Fold the other half of the scallop over so that the ham and cheese are enclosed. If you can, press the sides of the veal a little together; you don't want the ham and cheese to stick out on the sides. Dust the veal on both sides with flour, patting off any excess. Then dip it in the beaten egg so both sides are covered, then in the bread crumbs, again making sure both sides are well covered. Do this with all six of the veal scallops. Then put them on waxed paper in the refrigerator for about 30 minutes or longer to cool.

At serving time, heat the butter and vegetable oil in a heavy sautéing pan, add the veal packets, making sure they do not touch each other. (You will probably have to cook them in two batches.) Sauté them on each side until brown—about 1 to 2 minutes per side, no longer. Put them on a preheated serving platter, keeping them warm until all are cooked, and serve.

Yield: 6 servings

Hungarian Veal Ragout

The advantage of ragout-type dishes is that you can do them a day or two ahead of time or freeze them. In both cases, do not add the sour cream and heavy cream until serving time, as otherwise you might curdle the sour cream in the reheating process. I suggest that you serve noodles or spaetzle with this dish since they go particularly well with it. This is a great dish for a buffet-style dinner since it does not require a knife to eat it.

3	tablespoons butter
2	tablespoons vegetable oil
3	pounds shoulder of veal, cut into 1-inch cubes
2	onions, finely chopped
3	tablespoons all-purpose flour
2	tablespoons paprika
1	cup veal stock or chicken stock
1	cup white wine
	Salt and pepper to taste
1	cup sour cream
½	cup heavy cream
	Chopped fresh parsley

Heat the butter and vegetable oil in a heavy sautéing pan and brown the cubes of veal in it, making sure that they do not touch each other. You might have to do this in several batches. When all the veal is browned, put it aside and sauté the onions until lightly browned. Then add the flour and paprika, combining them well with the onions. Add the veal or chicken stock and the white wine. Season the sauce with salt and pepper, bring to a boil and add the browned veal. Lower the heat and simmer for about 1 to 1½ hours.

Just before serving, put the sour cream and heavy cream into a blender and add a little of your gravy. Blend well together. (This will make it easier to add the sour cream to the rest of your gravy without getting lumps.) After it is blended, add sour cream mixture to your sautéing pan and reheat gently without letting sauce come to a boil, as otherwise your sour cream will curdle. Put in a preheated serving dish and sprinkle some chopped parsley on top.

Yield: 6 servings

Veal Kidney with Mustard Cream

I adore veal kidneys and always find it very sad that more people in this country don't eat them. This is a great dish for brunch as well as a main course for dinner. Again, make sure not to overcook the kidneys because they will get tough.

2	pounds veal kidneys
1	tablespoon butter
2	tablespoons vegetable oil

Remove all membrane, fat and the white tubes from the kidneys and cut them into slices. Heat the butter and vegetable oil in a heavy sautéing pan, add the kidneys and sauté them over high heat for about 5 minutes. Then remove the kidneys and put aside. Add the onions to the

1	onion, finely chopped
2	tablespoons mustard (Dijon-style or Pommery)
2	tablespoons all-purpose flour
½	cup beef broth, double strength
	Salt and pepper to taste
½	cup heavy cream
	Chopped fresh parsley

pan and sauté until lightly browned. Add the mustard and flour, combining well with the onions. Then add the beef broth, bring to a boil, and return the kidneys to this sauce. Lower the heat and gently simmer for 5 minutes. Season the sauce with some salt and pepper, then add the heavy cream. Reheat without letting come to a boil. Put kidneys on a preheated platter and sprinkle some parsley on top.

Yield: 4 to 6 servings

Émincé of Veal

I had this dish for the first time in a very good restaurant in Switzerland. It was made right at the table. Along with it they served rösti, which is made from potatoes. It was an excellent meal, and I thoroughly enjoyed it. Émincé of Veal is so easy to make, it should definitely be in your repertoire. Here again, make sure that you do not overcook your veal. The whole dish shouldn't take more than about 6 minutes to prepare.

4	tablespoons butter
2	tablespoons vegetable oil
8	veal scallops, cut into thin strips
	Salt and pepper to taste
½	pound mushrooms, thinly sliced
2	tablespoons all-purpose flour
½	cup veal stock
¼	cup white wine
½	cup heavy cream

Heat the butter and vegetable oil in a heavy sautéing pan until very hot, then add the veal, seasoned with salt and pepper, stirring constantly with a spoon for about 2 minutes. (If your sautéing pan is small, you might have to do this in two batches.) Remove the veal and put aside, add the mushrooms to the sautéing pan and sauté them for about 1 minute. Sprinkle the flour over the mushrooms and combine well, then add the veal stock and white wine. Bring to a boil and cook on high heat for about 2 minutes. Add the heavy cream and veal. Reheat, making sure the sauce does not come to a boil. Serve immediately.

Yield: 4 to 6 servings

Tournedos Madagascar

This is a recipe that's easy and quick to do. I use the same recipe for a whole filet of beef, which I brown first in a sautéing pan and then roast in a 375°F. oven for 35 to 40 minutes, making the sauce in the pan in which I browned the filet. A tournedo, by the way, is simply a thick steak cut from the filet.

2   *tablespoons butter*

1   *tablespoon vegetable oil*

6   *tournedos of beef*

    Salt and pepper to taste

4   *shallots, finely chopped*

¾   *cup beef broth, double strength*

½   *cup dry red wine*

1   *teaspoon meat extract (Bovril)*

2   *tablespoons green peppercorns*

1   *teaspoon cornstarch mixed with a little water*

Heat the butter and oil in a heavy sautéing pan and add the tournedos, which you seasoned with salt and pepper, and brown them well on each side. Remove them from the pan and put aside. Add the shallots to the pan and sauté them for about 3 minutes. Add the beef broth, wine, meat extract and peppercorns, then simmer over low heat for about 10 minutes. Return the tournedos to this sauce and simmer to desired tenderness. Thicken the sauce with the cornstarch mixture and serve.

Yield: 6 servings

Note: Whenever you buy green peppercorns, make sure they are packed in brine or freeze-dried. The vinegar-packed ones are rather rubbery, and their taste is completely changed.

Filet of Beef in Aspic

This is not only the ultimate dish for a cold buffet or summer luncheon, but also a very convenient one since it can be made ahead of time. I generally serve Horseradish Cream or Mustard and Green Peppercorn Sauce with it, and a cold vegetable salad, such as Asparagus Vinaigrette.

1   *filet of beef*

    Salt and pepper to taste

2   *10½-ounce cans beef broth, double strength*

Preheat oven to 400°F., season the filet with salt and pepper, put in a roasting pan and roast in the oven for 40 minutes. Remove and cool; then wrap beef in foil and refrigerate, preferably overnight.

About 1 hour before slicing and assembling, make the aspic as follows. Put the beef broth, water and Madeira in a bowl. Sprinkle the gelatin in the ¼ cup water in a Pyrex

1   can water

½   cup Madeira

1½   packages (1½
     tablespoons)
     unflavored gelatin,
     dissolved in

¼   cup water

     Fresh watercress or
     parsley and

     Tomato roses, for
     decoration

measuring cup to soften, then dissolve; add it to the beef broth, water and Madeira mixture and cool in the refrigerator until aspic starts to thicken. Slice the beef into ¼-inch-thick slices. Cover the bottom of your serving platter with a little aspic, dip each slice of beef into the aspic lightly and arrange on platter. Put the platter into the refrigerator to jell further—about 1 hour—and decorate with watercress or parsley, and tomato roses.

Mustard and Green Peppercorn Sauce:

1   tablespoon green
     peppercorns

2   tablespoons Pommery
     mustard

½   cup vegetable oil

2   tablespoons olive oil

2   tablespoons cider
     vinegar

1   teaspoon honey

Combine all ingredients in a bowl with a whisk. Refrigerate for about 30 minutes before serving.

Horseradish Cream:

½   cup prepared white
     horseradish

1   cup heavy cream,
     whipped to soft peaks

     Salt and pepper to
     taste

Fold the horseradish into the whipped cream and season with salt and pepper.

Yield: 8 to 12 servings

Beef with Broccoli

This is one of my quick dishes for when I don't feel like standing in the kitchen for an hour. You can marinate and prepare all ingredients ahead of time and then just do the cooking, which goes very quickly. If you can't get broccoli, this is also great with zucchini or peppers.

2	cups flank steak, cut into oblong pieces about 1/8-inch thick
2	tablespoons soy sauce
2	tablespoons water
2	teaspoons cornstarch
1/2	cup vegetable oil
1	bunch broccoli, washed, cleaned and cut into flowerettes
2	tablespoons vegetable oil
2	tablespoons sherry
2	tablespoons water
	Salt and pepper to taste

Marinate the meat in the soy sauce, 2 tablespoons water, cornstarch and the 1/2 cup vegetable oil, all the ingredients well combined, for 30 minutes. Then quick-fry the broccoli in the 2 tablespoons vegetable oil, seasoning it with the sherry and adding 2 tablespoons water. Remove the broccoli and put aside. Then quick-fry the marinated beef in the same pan, stirring constantly. Add salt and pepper. Return the broccoli to the pan, combine well and serve.

Yield: 4 to 6 servings

Chicken

A chicken's tenderness depends on age, and its age relates directly to poundage. Thus, the more mature the bird, the more cooking or more thorough method of cooking it needs.

Broilers: Chickens of either sex that weigh from 1½ to 2½ pounds. They are used, as their name implies, for broiling.

Fryers: Chickens of either sex that weigh from 2½ to 3½ pounds. They are used for sautéing, poaching, baking or frying.

Roasters: Chickens of either sex that weigh from 3½ to 7 pounds. They are used for roasting with or without stuffing.

Capons: These are castrated male chickens, that weigh from 6 to 8 pounds. Their flesh is exceptionally tender, and they are usually also used for roasting.

To buy chicken, look for moist skin, a wing tip that yields readily if pressed back and a flexible breastbone. The color of the skin of the chicken, either white or yellow, is mainly due to the type of feed the chicken is fed, which depends upon the grower and area of the country in which it is raised. Remember, the taste of the chicken depends upon the quality of what it has been fed. So sales aren't always bargains. "You are what you eat" also applies to chickens.

Do not buy chickens that look dry, have a purplish color or broken or scaly skin.

When buying chicken that is in airtight wrap, make sure you remove the wrapping the minute you get home. Then wrap loosely, covering chicken completely but letting some air get in. Always keep chicken refrigerated.

If you want to freeze chicken, make sure you wrap it as tightly as possible (which goes for everything you freeze), the less air between the chicken and the wrapping the better. The slower you defrost your chicken before using, overnight in the refrigerator, for example, the less moisture loss you will have.

Roast Chicken

The one dish I always teach my New York classes to make is roast chicken. Everyone thinks they know how to make a roast chicken, but very few know how to make a good one. My method of sautéing the chicken first is a little more work, but your reward is a juicier, more appetizing and tastier bird.

1   *roasting chicken (about 5 pounds)*

    Salt and pepper to taste

1   *lemon, cut into slices*

1   *bunch of celery leaves*

3   *stalks parsley*

1   *teaspoon thyme*

4   *tablespoons butter*

4   *tablespoons vegetable oil*

1   *stalk celery, coarsely chopped*

1   *carrot, coarsely chopped*

1   *onion, coarsely chopped*

1   *bay leaf*

1   *teaspoon thyme*

1   *10½-ounce can chicken broth, double strength*

1   *cup dry white wine*

Preheat oven to 350°F. Season the chicken inside and out with salt and pepper, and stuff it with the lemon, celery leaves, parsley and 1 teaspoon thyme. Truss the chicken with cotton string. Heat the butter and oil in a heavy sautéing pan and brown the chicken well on all sides. Remove the browned chicken to a roasting pan. To the sautéing pan, add the chopped celery, carrot and onion, and sauté them over medium heat for about 5 minutes. Add the bay leaf, 1 teaspoon thyme, the chicken broth and wine, and bring to a boil. Pour this mixture over the chicken in the roasting pan and put in a 350°F. oven for 1 hour and 15 minutes. Baste the chicken about every 15 minutes.

Remove the chicken to a carving board, strain the sauce and thicken it with a little flour dissolved in water. Or if you like, you can put the sauce, unstrained—but remove the bay leaf—into a blender. This will give you a thicker sauce of the kind favored in what is referred to these days as the nouvelle cuisine.

Yield: 6 to 8 servings

Roast Chicken Archduke

If you think a roast chicken is a peasant dish, think again. This elegant dish has a stuffing and sauce fit for (at least) an archduke. The stuffing can also be used in crêpes, omelettes, or to fill artichoke bottoms as a first course. For a most impressive touch, put whole mushroom caps underneath the skin of the chicken.

1   *roasting chicken (about 5 pounds)*

    Salt and pepper to taste

4   *tablespoons butter*

2   *tablespoons vegetable oil*

First, make the filling. Put this stuffing into your chicken and truss it. Season it with salt and pepper. Heat the 4 tablespoons butter and the vegetable oil in a heavy sautéing pan and brown the chicken on all sides, keeping the heat on medium so as not to burn it. When the chicken is brown on all sides, flambé it with the calvados. (Be careful with this. Unless you have a perfectly clean hood over

Sauce:

¼ cup calvados (French
    apple brandy)

1   teaspoon beef extract
    (Bovril)

1   tablespoon tomato
    paste

2   tablespoons all-purpose
    flour

1   10½-ounce can
    chicken broth, double
    strength

¼ cup white wine

1   tablespoon dry sherry

1   tablespoon red currant
    jelly

    Salt and pepper to
    taste

Filling:

2   tablespoons butter

1   pound fresh mushrooms,
    thinly sliced

1   tablespoon lemon juice

4   ounces boiled ham,
    finely shredded

2   tablespoons dry sherry

1   teaspoon tarragon

1   small clove garlic, put
    through garlic press

    Salt and pepper to taste

1   tablespoon chopped
    parsley

4   ounces Gruyère cheese,
    finely shredded

your stove, flambé the chicken in the roasting pan, since the fat in the sautéing pan adds fuel.) Put the chicken in the roasting pan and add the rest of the sauce ingredients to your sautéing pan. Mix them well and bring to a boil, then pour over your chicken and roast it in a 350°F. oven for about 1 hour and 15 minutes. Baste your chicken with the sauce every 15 minutes.

Serve the chicken carved and the stuffing in the middle of the platter.

Yield: 6 to 8 servings

In a heavy sautéing pan, heat the 2 tablespoons butter and add the mushrooms, sautéing them for a few minutes. Sprinkle the lemon juice over them, then add the ham and sherry and stir, sautéing for one more minute. Then add the tarragon, garlic, salt, pepper and parsley, mix well, and take off the heat to cool. Then add the Gruyère cheese.

Chicken Pot Pie

This recipe has been kept secret for years. My former partner Joe and I developed the recipe some years ago when we opened a food take-out shop called The Great Take-Out. It was the specialty of the house and one of our biggest sellers. People would literally fly in from as far away as Los Angeles to get our pot pies. We would pack them in dry ice and off they went to the airport. In the last cookbook we published, we included the picture of the pot pie without the recipe. Well, this time the recipe is in. Although it involves several steps, the pie isn't difficult to make and the results are worth it. You can prepare it a day or two ahead of time and then just reheat it in a 350°F. oven or in a pinch you can even freeze it.

1	onion, coarsely chopped
1	carrot, coarsely chopped
1	stalk celery, coarsely chopped
	Bouquet garni (3 sprigs parsley, 2 celery leaves, 1 bay leaf, tied together with a cotton string)
6	peppercorns
	Salt to taste
1	roasting chicken (about 6 pounds)

Fill a large stockpot with water—you want enough water to cover your chicken. Add the onion, carrot, celery, bouquet garni, peppercorns, and salt and bring to a boil. Then add the chicken. (It stays juicier when you put it in boiling water. Only when making a chicken stock do you start your chicken in cold water.) Bring to a boil again, lower the heat, and simmer the chicken for about 1 hour. It is done when the leg comes off easily. Then put the chicken in a dish to cool. You can continue cooking your stock on high heat for another 15 minutes to make it richer. When the chicken is cool enough to handle, remove the skin and take the meat off the bones, cutting larger pieces such as the breast into about 1-inch squares. Then make the sauce.

Sauce:

4	tablespoons butter (unsalted)
4	tablespoons all-purpose flour
1½	cups chicken broth (use the stock from the pot in which you cooked the chicken)
1	tablespoon fresh lemon juice
	Salt and pepper to taste
½	cup heavy cream

Melt the butter in a heavy saucepan, add the flour, and cook, stirring constantly, for about 1 minute. Then add the chicken stock, stirring with a whisk until it comes to a boil, and simmer sauce for 5 minutes. Then add the lemon juice and salt and pepper. Lastly add the cream. Put the sauce aside while making your vegetables.

Vegetables:

3   *carrots, peeled and cut into ½-inch-thick slices*

1   *pound fresh mushrooms, thickly sliced*

2   *tablespoons butter*

1   *pound small white onions (you may use frozen thawed)*

1   *pound frozen small peas, thawed*

Simmer the carrots in about ½ cup water until tender but still crisp—about 10 minutes. Or you can steam them instead. Sauté the mushrooms in 2 tablespoons butter for about 5 minutes.

Assembling the Pot Pie. Put the chicken meat, carrots, mushrooms, thawed onions and peas in an ovenproof dish not more than 10 inches in diameter. Pour sauce over the chicken and vegetables.

Roll out the crust to a size to cover your baking dish. Sprinkle the grated cheese on top and roll over it one more time to incorporate the cheese into the crust. Make a hole in the middle of crust to let the steam escape. (I do this with a large plain round pastry tube.) Put crust on top of chicken, overlapping the sides of your dish, and brush with a mixture of egg yolk and 2 tablespoons heavy cream mixed together. Bake chicken pot pie in a pre-heated 375°F. oven for about 35 minutes or until the crust is golden brown.

Yield: 6 to 8 servings

Crust:

2   *cups all-purpose flour*

3   *ounces Crisco shortening*

3   *ounces butter*

⅓   *cup ice water*

1   *cup grated sharp Cheddar cheese*

1   *egg yolk*

2   *tablespoons heavy cream*

To make the crust, put the flour into a food processor or mixer. Add Crisco and butter (both should be very cold), and combine together. Then add the ice water and mix quickly until combined. Cool the crust in the refrigerator for at least 1 hour (or overnight if you want to do it ahead of time).

Broiled Chicken

Certainly one of the easiest ways to serve chicken is to broil it. Make sure your chicken does not weigh more than 2½ pounds. If the chicken is heavier than that, the skin will burn before the meat is completely cooked. When flavoring the chicken, as in this recipe with lemon juice and rosemary, let the bird marinate for at least 30 minutes. Lemon juice is a natural tenderizer and brings out the natural flavor. If you have to split the chicken yourself, simply cut out the backbone with kitchen scissors. Most herbs marry well with chicken, particularly tarragon, thyme and rosemary.

1   broiler (about 2½ pounds), split

Juice of 1 lemon

1   tablespoon rosemary

2   tablespoons softened butter or vegetable oil

Salt and pepper to taste

Sprinkle the chicken with the lemon juice and rub in well. Crush the rosemary in the palms of your hands (to release the volatile oils) and rub into the chicken. Do this at least 30 minutes before cooking. Preheat your broiler for about 5 minutes. Rub the chicken with butter or oil, then season with salt and pepper. Cook under broiler for about 15 minutes on each side, making sure not to burn the skin. Lower the broiler tray if necessary.

Yield: 2 servings

Broiler Chicken Japanese Style

I love soy sauce and use it a great deal. Use only a fine-quality soy sauce such as Kikkoman or Tamari. There are some American brands that are perfectly dreadful. The marinade in this recipe can also be used for pork or lamb.

½   cup soy sauce

1   clove garlic, put through garlic press

1   teaspoon grated fresh ginger or ½ teaspoon ground ginger

1   tablespoon honey

1   tablespoon vegetable oil

Juice of 1 lemon

1   broiler (about 2½ pounds), split

Combine all ingredients except the chicken in a bowl, mix well, pour over the chicken, coating both sides, and allow to marinate for at least 30 minutes. Preheat broiler for 5 minutes and cook chicken about 15 minutes on each side. Lower the broiler tray if necessary, to be sure the chicken does not burn.

Yield: 2 servings

Chicken Vinaigre

3 tablespoons vegetable oil

1 chicken (about 3 pounds), cut into eighths

Salt and pepper to taste

1 ounce calvados (French apple brandy)

2 tablespoons finely chopped shallots

2 apples, peeled, cored and sliced

½ cup dry white wine

½ cup chicken broth, double strength

¼ cup cider vinegar

1 teaspoon honey

1 tablespoon Pommery mustard

Freshly chopped parsley

Heat the oil in a heavy sautéing pan. Add the chicken, which has been seasoned with salt and pepper, and sauté until brown on all sides.

Heat the calvados and pour, flaming, over the chicken. Since the fat will feed the flames, only do this if you have a clean metal exhaust hood over your stove or high ceilings. Also make sure to stand back. (Or you can remove the chicken from the pan, put it on a heatproof platter and pour the ignited calvados over it.) When the flame burns out, remove the chicken from the sautéing pan and put aside. Add the shallots and apples to the pan and sauté until brown. Add the wine, chicken broth, vinegar, honey and mustard.

Return the chicken to the pan, bring to a boil and simmer gently for 30 minutes. Put the chicken on a preheated serving platter and put the sauce in the blender and blend until smooth. Then pour the sauce over the chicken and sprinkle with parsley.

Yield: 4 to 6 servings

Chicken Paprikash

This is a recipe I did for Better Homes and Gardens *a few years ago, and I received hundreds of letters from grateful readers, so I think you'll enjoy it. As I will point out again in the recipe for Loin of Pork Paprikash, you must have real Hungarian paprika.*

3   tablespoons vegetable oil

1   chicken (about 3 pounds), cut into eighths

    Salt and pepper to taste

2   medium-size yellow onions, chopped

1   tablespoon paprika

½   cup dry white wine

½   cup chicken broth, double strength

1   cup sour cream

    Chopped fresh parsley, for decoration

Heat the vegetable oil in a heavy sautéing pan. Add the chicken, which has been seasoned with salt and pepper, and sauté until brown on all sides. Remove the chicken from the pan and put aside. Add the onions to the pan and sauté them until lightly browned. Then add the paprika, combining it well with the onions. Return the chicken to the pan and add the wine and chicken broth. Bring to a boil and simmer gently for about 30 to 35 minutes. Just before serving, remove the chicken and add the sour cream, making sure not to let the sauce come to a boil, otherwise, the sour cream will curdle. Pour this sauce over the chicken and sprinkle parsley on top.

Serve with wide noodles or gnocchi.

Yield: 4 to 6 servings

Note: If you put the sour cream in a blender or food processor and add a little of the sauce and blend for a few seconds, it will be easier to mix it into the rest of the sauce without getting lumps.

Lemon Chicken

3   whole chicken breasts, skinned, boned and cut in half

    Juice of 1 lemon

1   teaspoon grated fresh ginger or ¼ teaspoon ground ginger

1   clove garlic, put through garlic press

2   tablespoons cornstarch

1   tablespoon vegetable oil

1   tablespoon water

2   tablespoons vegetable oil

Cut the chicken breasts into thin strips, put into a bowl and add the lemon juice, ginger, garlic, cornstarch, 1 tablespoon vegetable oil and the water. Combine all these ingredients and let marinate for about 10 minutes.

Heat the 2 tablespoons vegetable oil in a heavy sautéing pan. When oil is very hot, add drained snowpeas or broccoli, season with salt and pepper, and stir constantly for 2 minutes. Then remove and put aside. Add marinated chicken breasts to the hot pan, season with salt and pepper and stir constantly for about 3 minutes. Then add chicken broth, bring to a boil, add snowpeas or broccoli, combine and serve.

Yield: 4 to 6 servings

1 pound snowpeas,
cleaned and left in ice
water for 5 minutes or

1 head of broccoli, peeled
and cut up

Salt and pepper to taste

1 cup chicken broth,
double strength

Chicken Breasts in Champagne

There are countless recipes using skinned and boned chicken breasts, and there isn't any reason why you shouldn't create some of your own. All the major poultry growers sell them. They are called chicken cutlets. Although I always try to cook with fresh chicken, I do keep a quantity of cutlets in my freezer, individually wrapped, for emergencies. They are particularly good for stir-frying with almost any vegetable. The main thing to remember about chicken breasts is not to overcook them.

3 whole chicken breasts, boned, skinned and cut in half

Juice of 1 lemon

1 teaspoon thyme

Salt and pepper to taste

4 tablespoons butter

1 tablespoon vegetable oil

½ cup shallots, finely chopped

2 cups fresh mushrooms, thinly sliced

½ cup champagne

½ cup chicken broth, double strength

2 tablespoons parsley, finely chopped

1 teaspoon all-purpose flour mixed with

1 teaspoon butter

Sprinkle the chicken with lemon juice and thyme and let marinate for 5 minutes. Then season with salt and pepper.

In a heavy sautéing pan, heat the butter and oil and brown the chicken breasts on both sides. Remove from the pan and put aside. Add the shallots and mushrooms to the pan and sauté for about 4 minutes, stirring constantly. Then add the champagne and chicken broth; simmer this sauce for 10 minutes. Add the parsley and thicken sauce with the flour and butter mixture.

Yield: 6 servings

Cornish Hens

Cornish Hens make a very elegant main course, and I love the delicate taste of these birds. Try to get fresh ones. They are much better than the frozen ones. Prepare one hen per person. I serve them usually on a large round platter in a circle, and decorate the middle with a bunch of fresh watercress and surround them with carrots and grapes as vegetables.

6	Cornish hens
	Salt and pepper to taste
2	tablespoons butter
2	tablespoons vegetable oil
1	carrot, coarsely chopped
1	stalk celery, coarsely chopped
1	onion, coarsely chopped
1	bay leaf
1	teaspoon thyme
1	cup dry white wine
1	10½-ounce can chicken broth, double strength

Prepare the stuffing first. Season the Cornish hens with salt and pepper, and stuff. Truss the birds with cotton string. In a heavy sautéing pan, heat the butter and vegetable oil, then brown the Cornish hens on all sides, keeping the heat medium high. When they are brown all over, put in a roasting pan. Then add the carrot, celery and onion to the sautéing pan, and sauté them for about 5 minutes. Add the bay leaf, thyme, wine and chicken broth. Bring this to a boil and pour over the Cornish hens, into the roasting pan. Put in a preheated 350°F. oven for about 45 minutes. Baste about every 10 minutes.

Before serving, strain and thicken the sauce with a little flour if you wish.

Yield: 6 servings

Stuffing:

6	slices stale white bread
1	can chicken broth, double strength
3	eggs, lightly beaten
1	tablespoon thyme
½	cup chopped parsley
½	tablespoon marjoram
1	teaspoon summer savory
	Salt and pepper to taste

Soak the bread in the chicken broth for a few minutes. Squeeze dry with your fingers and crumble it. Add the eggs and the rest of the ingredients. Mix well.

Roast Duck Madagascar

Although this recipe is in my second cookbook, I feel justified in repeating it for those people who don't have that book, because this recipe is too good to miss. I suggest that you serve about one-quarter duck per person.

A perfectly cooked duck should have a crunchy crisp skin, but the meat should be tender and moist. That is why I object to the traditional method of pricking the skin to release the fat. This works well enough on the fat, but too much of the meat juice is lost at the same time. This method of cooking the duck in a very hot oven for one hour will release the fat yet keep the meat juices intact.

Green peppercorns are an integral part of this great dish, and you can find them in cans in most fine food shops. Make sure to get a brand packed in water rather than vinegar. Green peppercorns are peppercorns that have been picked before they have completely ripened and while they are still soft.

2 *Long Island ducklings (about 5 pounds)*

Salt and pepper to taste

1 *orange, cut into 4 pieces*

2 *celery leaves*

1 *medium onion, cut into quarters*

4 *sprigs parsley*

Preheat oven to 450°F. Rub the ducks inside and out with salt and pepper. Stuff with orange, celery leaves, onion and parsley. Close the openings with metal skewers and put the ducks on their backs on a rack in a roasting pan. Put about ½ inch of water in the roasting pan to catch the fat (instead of smoking up your kitchen). Roast the ducks for 30 minutes, then turn them over and continue roasting for another 30 minutes. While the ducks are in the oven, make the stock.

Stock:

1 *medium onion, cut in half*

1 *stalk celery with leaves*

1 *carrot, chopped*

2 *sprigs parsley*

1 *bay leaf*

5 *peppercorns*

1 *teaspoon salt*

2 *cups red wine*

1 *cup water*

2 *tablespoons all-purpose flour or 1 tablespoon cornstarch mixed with*

2 *tablespoons butter*

Giblets of duck

2 *tablespoons green peppercorns (the variety packed in water, not vinegar)*

Put all the stock ingredients except the green peppercorns in a heavy saucepan. Bring to a boil and simmer for 1 hour. Then put the stock through a strainer and add green peppercorns.

Remove the ducks from the oven and discard the fat and water in the roasting pan. Reduce the oven temperature to 375°F. Pour the stock and green peppercorns over the ducks and return them to the oven. Continue roasting the ducks for another hour, basting every 10 minutes.

When done, place the ducks on a serving platter and thicken the sauce with the flour and butter mixture. Serve the sauce on the side.

Yield: 6 to 8 servings

Pork

Pork is a much more popular meat in Germany and Central European countries and even in China than here in the United States. This fact is gradually changing due to the high price of beef and lamb compared to pork and because farmers are producing leaner hogs, which are better suited to the new lower-in-fat American diet.

Lack of experience has caused most Americans to badly overcook pork to the point where it is completely dry and tasteless. To avoid any danger of trichinosis, pork must be thoroughly cooked, but this can be way overdone. Up until recent years, it was generally accepted that pork should have an internal temperature of 185°F. to be safe. Some recent studies have put that figure at 170°F. You can make those decisions yourself, or you can test the juices by sticking a fork into your roast. When the juice runs white instead of pink, the roast should be done. By all means be safe, but don't cook your pork to death.

Loin of Pork Stuffed with Apricots and Prunes

This is one of the most popular pork dishes I serve. Pork and fruit have a natural affinity, as you will see when you taste this dish. When cooking a pork loin, I always have the butcher bone it and give me the bones, which I cook in the sauce. It makes a delicious lunch the next day. A boned loin is much easier to brown and slice. To stuff a loin, you can either push a long honing steel through the meat lengthwise to create a sort of tunnel, or you can make a long, deep cut, fill it and then tie up the meat with string.

1   *loin of pork (4 to 5 pounds), boned*

1   *pound dried apricots, soaked in water*

½   *pound dried prunes, soaked in water*

    Salt and pepper to taste

1   *tablespoon rosemary*

3   *tablespoons vegetable oil*

1   *large onion, chopped*

3   *apples (Granny Smith or other tart variety), peeled, cored and coarsely chopped*

1   *10½-ounce can chicken broth, double strength*

1   *cup dry white wine*

½   *tablespoon cornstarch mixed in a little water*

Stuff the loin of pork with half the apricots and all the prunes. Season with salt and pepper and rub well with the rosemary. Heat the vegetable oil in a heavy sautéing pan and brown the loin well on all sides. Remove from pan, pour off excess fat and add the onion and apples to the sautéing pan. Sauté them until lightly browned, then add the rest of the apricots, chicken broth, wine and the pork. Bring sauce to a boil, cover, lower heat and simmer for 1½ hours.

Remove loin to a carving board and thicken your sauce with the cornstarch dissolved in a little water. Slice the pork, put it on a preheated serving platter and pour some of the sauce on top.

Yield: 6 servings

Loin of Pork Paprikash

Like the Germans, Hungarians love pork, and more particularly, pork with paprika. Most Americans think of paprika as something to decorate food, like parsley. But Hungarian paprika is entirely different. It is full bodied and robust and can be very hot, like cayenne pepper. The world's finest paprika comes from an area around Szeged in Hungary, where they produce many varieties from mild to very hot.

I can get very carried away talking about things like great paprika, and I usually do, which gets me into no end of trouble. A few years ago, I started to make paprika dishes in my travels around the country, and the next thing I knew, I was promising to send all my students paprika from New York. This sort of got out of hand, and I ended up with a mail-order business run out of the Cookingschool. And to this day, you're likely to find huge sacks of paprika or peppercorns all over the place, waiting to be packed in little plastic bags and sent around the country. I just can't seem to keep quiet.

At any rate, good Hungarian paprika is really great. Always store it in the refrigerator to preserve the flavor and color. And never sauté your paprika because the natural sugar will caramelize and discolor as well as change flavor.

1	loin of pork (about 4 to 5 pounds), boned
	Salt and pepper to taste
3	tablespoons vegetable oil
2	yellow onions, chopped
2	red peppers, coarsely chopped
2	green peppers, coarsely chopped
1	clove garlic, put through a garlic press
2	tablespoons paprika
3	tablespoons all-purpose flour
2	10½-ounce cans chicken broth, double strength
1	can water
½	cup sour cream

Season the loin of pork with salt and pepper. In a heavy sautéing pan heat the oil, add the pork and brown on all sides. Remove the pork and put aside, add the onions to the sautéing pan and sauté until lightly browned. Then add the peppers and garlic and continue sautéing for another few minutes. Add the paprika and flour and combine well. Add chicken broth and water, bring to a boil and return the browned loin of pork to this. Cover and simmer for about 1½ hours.

Remove the pork and slice. Add the sour cream to the sauce and combine well. Make sure not to let it come to a boil. Serve the sauce separately.

This dish can also be made with a loin of veal, or with pork chops in which case you simply cut down the cooking time to about 35 minutes, depending on the thickness of the chops.

Yield: 8 servings

Moo Shu Pork

I have always loved this dish, and I was thrilled when Dee Wang taught my students how to make it. Now I make it when my craving for it gets out of hand, but usually hope that whenever Dee comes to visit me she will bring me some that she made that morning. She knows of my passion for it, and I am not above asking her for it.

1	*cup lean pork shoulder, shredded*
2	*tablespoons soy sauce*
1	*teaspoon cornstarch*
½	*cup corn oil (approximately), for stir-frying*
1½	*cups cabbage, finely shredded*
30	*tiger-lily buds, soaked and cut*
½	*cup cloud ears, soaked*
1	*tablespoon vegetable oil*
3	*eggs*
1	*tablespoon chicken broth*
1–2	*tablespoons soy sauce, optional*
2	*teaspoons sesame-seed oil, optional*
4	*scallions, sliced*

Marinate the pork with 2 tablespoons soy sauce and the cornstarch. Stir-fry the cabbage, then add tiger-lily buds and cloud ears and cook 2 minutes. Remove to a plate. Stir-fry the pork, then add vegetables.

Put 1 tablespoon vegetable oil in a separate pan and scramble the eggs, which have been beaten together with chicken broth. Add to the pork and vegetables. Add more soy sauce, if desired, and top with the sliced scallions. Sesame-seed oil can be added with the soy sauce. Serve with Mandarin Pancakes. Or put this mixture over Chinese noodles and you have great lo mein.

Yield: 6 servings of 2 filled pancakes each

Mandarin Pancakes:

½	*cup boiling water less 2 tablespoons*
1	*teaspoon salt*
1	*cup all-purpose flour*
1	*tablespoon corn oil*

Pour boiling water onto salt and flour, stir and knead with additional flour until not sticky in the hands.

Rest dough for about 10 minutes, then separate into twelve round balls. Flatten each ball to a 2½-inch round and sandwich two pieces of dough together with corn oil to make six rounds. Roll out rounds until very thin. Heat each round in an ungreased frying pan until air bubbles appear. Turn. Remove from pan. Separate the two halves by slitting edge with a sharp knife. Stack and steam in aluminum foil.

Yield: 12 pancakes

Note: Chinese groceries and specialty shops can supply delicacies such as tiger-lily buds and cloud ears.

Loin of Pork with Sauerkraut

This is definitely a German dish and a great one. It's easy to make, and on a cold winter day, the aroma of it cooking fills your home.

My favorite sauerkraut is Hengstenberg, which is made in Germany not far from my hometown and packed in white wine. It's so good, you can eat it right out of the can. If you buy some, don't rinse out the wine.

1   loin of pork (about 4 to 5 pounds)

    Salt and pepper to taste

3   tablespoons vegetable oil

2   yellow onions, chopped

2   28¾-ounce cans of sauerkraut (Hengstenberg)

2   cups white wine

1   bay leaf

5   juniper berries

1   Golden Delicious apple, peeled, cored and cut in cubes

Season the loin of pork with salt and pepper. In a heavy sautéing pan, heat the oil, add the pork and brown on all sides. Remove the pork and put aside. Add the onions to the sautéing pan and sauté until lightly browned. Then add the rest of the ingredients. Bring to a boil and return the browned loin of pork to the pan. Cover and simmer for about 1½ hours.

Remove the pork and slice. Put on a preheated serving platter and surround with the sauerkraut.

Yield: 8 servings

Fish

Fish is my favorite food. Unfortunately, too few people know how to handle it properly, and overcooking fish is probably the most common mistake people make. Although fish has gotten very expensive, it's well worth it if you consider the fact that you have very little or no waste when cooking it. When buying fish, make sure you go to a good fish market. If you can smell the store a block away, stay away, since fresh fish does not smell. Of course, there are the usual signs to look for—clear eyes and good red gills—but your best guide to freshness is your nose. Being a great aficionado of sashimi and sushi, which is raw fish, I can tell you that fresh fish does not smell or taste unpleasant. Once you have bought your fish, always keep it refrigerated until you are ready to use it. The following recipes give you just a small sample of all the things you can do with fish; so once you have learned the basics, go ahead and create.

Broiled Fish

Broiling is probably one of the most popular ways to cook fish. So let me give you some basic rules for broiling fish. Sprinkle the filet with fresh lemon juice. This will not only make it more flavorful, but will also give it firmer texture. Then season it with salt and pepper. Butter an ovenproof dish to fit the fish. This will make it easier to remove the cooked fish and clean the dish. Lay the filet in the dish and fold the tail end—the narrow, thin end—under, to assure that the fish cooks evenly. Put a few dots of butter on it, if you like, and place in a preheated broiler as close to the flame as possible without burning the fish. Depending upon your broiler, it should take 2 to 5 minutes to cook. You do not turn the fish; you broil just one side. Remember, if your fish is too far from the broiler flames, you will end up simply baking the fish. Many ovens have doors on the broiler that will stay ajar during broiling to prevent heat buildup. If you have large, thick filets, such as striped bass, obviously the broiling time is a little longer, but please, don't overcook fish. Whenever you are not sure whether the fish is done, simply take a fork and insert it into the filet. If the flesh flakes and is white (not translucent) it is done.

Baked Filet of Sole Celestine

The shrimp filling for this recipe can also be used to stuff whole fish, such as trout or red snapper. It can be made ahead of time and refrigerated. I find it's also marvelous rolled in crêpes.

6   *filets of sole*
    Juice of 1 lemon
    Salt and pepper to taste

Filling:

2   *tablespoons butter*

1   *tablespoon vegetable oil*

1   *bunch scallions, cleaned and finely chopped*

1   *red pepper*

1   *pound shrimp, cleaned and coarsely chopped*
    Juice of 1 lemon
    Salt and pepper to taste

Sprinkle the filets of sole with lemon juice and season with salt and pepper.

In a heavy sautéing pan, heat the butter and oil, add the scallions and red pepper and sauté for a few minutes without letting brown. Then add the shrimp, season with lemon juice and salt and pepper and sauté for about 3 minutes. Add the bread crumbs, combine well and put aside to cool for a few minutes. Preheat oven to 350°F.

Take a round gratin dish, drape the filets over the edge of the dish in a circle so that one-half of each is in the pan with the tail, or small end, toward the center of the dish. Cover the half of each filet that is in the dish with the filling and fold the other half over it. Pour the wine over fish, cover with aluminum foil and put into preheated oven for 20 minutes.

Transfer the filet of sole to a preheated serving platter and thicken sauce with 1 tablespoon softened butter and 1 tablespoon flour combined. Pour sauce over fish and serve.

Yield: 6 servings

3 tablespoons bread
crumbs

¼ cup dry white wine

1 tablespoon butter,
softened

1 tablespoon all-purpose
flour

Fish with Ginger Sauce

With her kind permission, I have adopted this recipe from Dee Wang, a good friend of mine for many years, whom I consider one of the most effective teachers of Chinese cooking in the field today. She believes, as I do, that all great recipes are simple and only bad cooks make them complicated. I would love to include her recipe for Peking Duck, but even I haven't mastered that one yet.

2 scallions

⅓ cup soy sauce

⅓ cup chicken broth,
double strength

½ teaspoon sugar

⅓ cup water

1 teaspoon cornstarch
mixed with

1 tablespoon water

2 tablespoons corn oil

2 tablespoons finely
shredded fresh ginger

4 cups water

1 teaspoon salt

1½ pounds of fish filets
(haddock, flounder or
sole, preferably fresh,
not frozen), cut into
4-inch pieces

Chop scallions, keeping white and green parts separate. Mix soy sauce, chicken broth, sugar and ⅓ cup water. Add cornstarch mixed with 1 tablespoon water.

Heat corn oil in a small saucepan. Add scallion whites and ginger and cook until light brown. Add soy-sauce mixture and bring to a boil. Thicken with cornstarch mixture and keep the sauce warm.

Bring the 4 cups of water to a boil, add the salt and regulate the heat to keep the water simmering. Drop the pieces of fish into the water. When the fish becomes flaky, lift out the pieces with a slotted spoon and arrange on a serving dish. Pour the sauce over fish and serve garnished with the scallion greens.

Yield: 4 to 6 servings

Steamed Filet of Fish

If I ever had to choose just one cuisine to eat for the rest of my life, it would be Japanese. There is nobody who can make as much from less or make it look and taste like more than the Japanese. I am convinced this is where the French learned about cuisine minceur and nouvelle cuisine. When I cook fish for myself, I often choose this dish because it has a very clean and fresh taste. The scallions, carrot and dill are mainly for looks, as steamed fish all by itself doesn't look that exciting.

2   slices filet of sole, flounder or fluke

Fresh lemon juice

2   scallions, cleaned and each cut diagonally into 4 pieces

8   thin slices of carrot

8   tiny sprigs of fresh dill or parsley

Salt and pepper to taste or Spike seasoning

Put the fish filets in an ovenproof dish, such as a Pyrex pie plate. Sprinkle them with lemon juice and put the strips of scallions crosswise on the fish. Then put 1 slice of carrot on each in the middle and, behind each carrot slice, the sprig of dill or parsley. Season with salt and pepper or a little Spike. If you have a large steamer, simply stand the dish in it and steam fish for 3 to 5 minutes. Or create a steamer, using a 12-inch sautéing pan. Put stainless-steel tongs in the bottom of the pan, and fill the pan with about 1 inch of cold water. Stand your Pyrex plate on top of the tongs, bring the water in the pan to a boil, then cover the pan and steam the fish for about 3 to 5 minutes, depending on the thickness of the filets.

Yield: 2 servings

Fluke Japanese Style

I would like to leave you with one thought about fish. Japanese cuisine has been dominated by fish for centuries. The Japanese are artists in preparing it. They eat almost all varieties raw with the most delicate seasoning. When they cook fish, it is only for the briefest time. This dish was made for me by my favorite sushi chef. It's so simple, it's not even a recipe, but it was superb. I don't think anything in this world as marvelous as fresh fish needs flour and cream all over it.

6   slices of fluke filet

Fresh lemon juice

2   tablespoons soy sauce

Pour the lemon juice and soy sauce over the fish. Put under a preheated broiler for 3 to 5 minutes. Then serve.

Yield: 6 servings

Note: If fluke is not available, 2 pounds bay scallops may be substituted.

Sautéed Almond Sole

The filet is pan-fried over very high heat to seal in the moisture and create a crunchy shell. I love the contrast between the tender flaky fish inside and the browned almonds. Try cooking your next fish dinner using this method; believe me, it will be a big hit. Try not to make it for more than six people unless you use two huge sautéing pans, because it should be served right off the fire.

6 filets of sole, flounder or fluke

Fresh lemon juice

Salt and pepper to taste

1 cup all-purpose flour

3 egg whites, lightly beaten

2 cups finely chopped almonds

4 tablespoons butter

4 tablespoons vegetable oil

Sprinkle the filets with lemon juice and season them with salt and pepper. Then dip them in the flour, shaking to remove any excess. (You just want to dust them.) Afterwards, dip into egg whites on both sides and then into almonds, patting to cover well. Remove to a rack or waxed paper and allow to dry for at least 10 minutes. Or you can do this several hours ahead of time, keeping the filets on a waxed-paper-covered cookie sheet in the refrigerator.

Heat butter and oil in a heavy sautéing pan. When very hot, add the filets and cook for 1 or 2 minutes on each side or until they are nicely browned. Make sure they do not touch each other in the pan.

Serve with a wedge of fresh lemon and a nice green salad.

Yield: 6 servings

Whole Cold Striped Bass

You may wonder why I have not mentioned a fish poacher. It's simply because I don't think they are necessary. If you cook whole fish frequently, they can be convenient, but only if easy to clean. I find the ones lined with tin very difficult to clean, and, since I always poach fish with white wine, aluminum is out. I own several fish poachers, which I find make great centerpieces for buffets filled with flowers.

1	whole striped bass (about 6 pounds), cleaned
2	cups white wine
1	cup water
1	onion, chopped
½	lemon, sliced
1	bay leaf
1	stalk celery with leaf, chopped
2	sprigs parsley
5	peppercorns
1	carrot, cut up
1	teaspoon salt

Rinse fish well in cold water and pat dry. Wrap in cheesecloth and place in a shallow baking pan.

In a large saucepan, combine remaining ingredients and bring to a boil. Reduce the heat and simmer for 15 minutes. Pour this stock over the fish. Cover baking pan with aluminum foil. Put in a preheated 350°F. oven for about 35 to 40 minutes.

Remove fish from the oven and place carefully on a platter. Remove skin, cover fish with plastic wrap and refrigerate. When cold, decorate. Serve fish with Sauce Gribiche.

Yield: 8 servings

Sauce Gribiche

Sauce Gribiche is basically a form of mayonnaise. If you have a food processor this is a snap, but making mayonnaise without one is quite simple if you remember that the oil must be added extremely slowly, drop by drop in the beginning. As the eggs begin to absorb the oil, you can increase the amounts gradually. If the mayonnaise does not thicken, you have added the oil too fast. For best results, have all ingredients at room temperature.

2	large egg yolks
2	dashes cayenne pepper
1	tablespoon Dijon-style mustard
¾	cup olive oil
¾	cup vegetable oil

2	tablespoons vinegar or lemon juice	Put the egg yolks, cayenne and mustard in the bowl of an electric mixer; beat well. At low speed, gradually add the oil until it is all absorbed and the mixture has thickened. Slowly add the vinegar or lemon juice, then add the rest of the ingredients and mix well. Keep in the refrigerator until ready to use.

2   tablespoons vinegar or lemon juice

½   cup chopped sour pickles

1   tablespoon chopped parsley

1   tablespoon chopped chervil

1   tablespoon chopped chives

1   tablespoon chopped fresh tarragon or ½ tablespoon dried

2   hard-boiled eggs, put through a strainer

    Salt and pepper to taste

Put the egg yolks, cayenne and mustard in the bowl of an electric mixer; beat well. At low speed, gradually add the oil until it is all absorbed and the mixture has thickened. Slowly add the vinegar or lemon juice, then add the rest of the ingredients and mix well. Keep in the refrigerator until ready to use.

Yield: 2 cups

Salmon Trout Farci en Papillote

This recipe is also very good with red snapper. If you do not like the taste of anisette, you can simply leave it out. The stuffing can be made ahead of time and refrigerated.

1   salmon trout (about 6 pounds)

    Lemon juice

    Salt and pepper to taste

2   tablespoons butter

½   pound mushrooms, thinly sliced

1   cup thinly sliced scallions

1   tablespoon chopped dill

1   tablespoon anisette, optional

½   cup bread crumbs

    Parchment paper or aluminum foil

Preheat oven to 350°F. Season the salmon trout with lemon juice, salt and pepper.

In a heavy sautéing pan, heat butter, add mushrooms and scallions, and sauté for about 3 minutes without letting them brown. Then add the dill, anisette and bread crumbs and continue sautéing for another minute, combining well. Cool this stuffing for a while.

Put your fish on the parchment paper or aluminum foil, then fill it with cooled stuffing. Fold parchment paper or aluminum foil and close up tightly. Put the fish in a gratin dish or roasting pan and bake for about 35 minutes.

At serving time, cut open the parchment or foil in the middle and serve.

Yield: 4 to 6 servings

Whole Salmon in Aspic

This will always be the crowning glory of any buffet, so you may be surprised that the recipe is so short. I have made it so many hundreds of times, I know it needn't be complicated. When ordering the salmon, ask your fish man to remove the center bone, leaving the fish whole. This makes it a lot easier to serve. Having the head removed is a matter of preference for decorating. If you don't like aspic, simply eliminate it. The same recipe can be used for whole striped bass and salmon trout.

1	whole salmon (about 6 pounds), cleaned and pan dressed
2	cups white wine
1	cup water
1	onion, chopped
½	lemon, sliced
1	bay leaf
1	stalk celery with leaf, chopped
2	sprigs parsley
5	peppercorns
1	carrot, cut up
1	teaspoon salt
1	package unflavored gelatin, softened

Preheat oven to 350° F. Rinse the fish well in cold water and pat dry. Wrap it in cheesecloth and place in a shallow baking pan. (The cheesecloth will enable you to lift the fish from the pan without fear of breaking it).

In a large saucepan, combine the remaining ingredients, except the gelatin, and bring to a boil. Reduce heat and simmer for 15 minutes. Pour this stock over fish, and cover pan with aluminum foil. Put fish into preheated 350° F. oven for 35 minutes. Remove fish from the oven and place carefully on a platter. Remove the top skin, cover fish with plastic wrap and refrigerate until very cold. Put the stock through a strainer and add softened gelatin; refrigerate until it just starts to thicken. Cover salmon with this aspic and return to the refrigerator. When aspic is set, decorate salmon with parsley, lemon and tomatoes. Serve with Sauce Gribiche (see page 90) or Sauce Verte.

Yield: 6 to 8 servings

Sauce Verte:

2	large egg yolks
2	dashes cayenne pepper
1	tablespoon Dijon-style mustard
¾	cup olive oil
¾	cup vegetable oil
2	tablespoons vinegar or lemon juice
1	tablespoon parsley, finely chopped
2	tablespoons watercress, finely chopped

With a food processor, this recipe is easy. If you don't have one, put egg yolks, cayenne and mustard in the bowl of an electric mixer; beat well. At a low speed, very gradually add oil until all is absorbed and the mixture has thickened. Then slowly add vinegar or lemon juice. Add the rest of the ingredients and mix well. Keep in the refrigerator until ready to use.

Yield: 2 cups

2   tablespoons chervil,
    finely chopped

2   tablespoons finely
    chopped fresh tarragon
    or 1 tablespoon dried

1   tablespoon cooked
    spinach, put through a
    sieve

    Salt and pepper to
    taste

Cold Salmon Mousse

You won't often find a food processor mentioned in this book, but I give that machine four stars when I make this mousse. The recipe below is for the old-fashioned method, in which you have your fish man grind the salmon for you twice and then you make the mousse using an electric mixer. The second, food-processor method, is the ultimate in simplicity. This mousse can also be served hot with a mousseline sauce or in individual timbales.

    Vegetable oil

1½ pounds salmon,
    skinned, boned and
    put through the
    grinder twice

2   egg whites

1½ cups light cream

2   teaspoons salt

3   shakes cayenne pepper

¼   teaspoon ground
    cardamom seeds

Preheat oven to 350° F. Take an 8-inch ring mold and wipe it well with some oil. Put the ground salmon into the bowl of an electric mixer and add egg whites. Mix well. Then add light cream very slowly, still mixing. When all cream has been added, season with the salt (which will also thicken the mousse), cayenne and cardamom. Lightly press the mousse into the oiled mold, cover with aluminum foil and stand the mold in a shallow pan half-filled with hot water. Put into a preheated 350° F. oven for 25 minutes.

Remove from the oven and cool, then cover mold with plastic wrap and chill in the refrigerator until cold.

To unmold the mousse, run a knife just around the top to loosen, and turn mold upside down on your serving platter. Put some watercress in the middle and serve with Sauce Gribiche (see page 90).

Food-Processor Method:

1½ pounds salmon,
    skinned, boned and
    cut into chunks

    All other ingredients
    are the same as above

Put salmon into your food processor and process for 20 seconds. Then add egg whites and process for another 20 seconds before adding the light cream in a thin stream. When all the cream has been added, add the rest of the ingredients and follow the above recipe for cooking.

Yield: 12 servings

Scallop Mousse

Whenever I serve this mousse, it is a smash hit! It will establish you as a star, too, as long as you don't tell anyone how easy it is to make. Here again is where you start getting some of your money back from the food processor.

If you can find a really good tomato, peel it, remove the seeds, and cut it into thin strips. Add it to the sauce at the last minute.

2   *pounds bay scallops*

2   *egg yolks*

2   *cups heavy cream*

    Salt and pepper to taste

Sauce:

2   *tablespoons butter*

2   *tablespoons shallots, finely chopped*

½   *cup dry white wine*

    Salt and pepper to taste

1   *cup heavy cream*

½   *tablespoon cornstarch mixed with*

3   *tablespoons water*

1   *tablespoon fresh parsley, finely chopped*

1   *large tomato, peeled and sliced, optional*

Preheat oven to 375° F. Reserve 1 cup of scallops for the sauce and put the remaining scallops in your food processor. Blend for about 30 seconds. Then add egg yolks and blend well. Slowly add the 2 cups of heavy cream; season with salt and pepper. Butter a ring mold well and fill with the scallop mousse. Put in a pan filled with hot water and bake in a preheated 375° F. oven for 40 minutes.

In the meantime, make the sauce. Melt the butter in a sautéing pan, add shallots and sauté for a few minutes. Then add wine. Bring to a boil and simmer for about 10 minutes and add the 1 cup of scallops. Season them with salt and pepper, bring to a boil, lower the heat and simmer about 1 minute. Then add the 1 cup heavy cream, heat and add the cornstarch mixture, but do not let sauce boil. Serve this sauce over the scallop mousse. Garnish with parsley.

Yield: 12 servings

Sautéed Soft-Shell Crabs

Every year around May, the soft-shell crab season starts on the east coast, and I can hardly wait. Contrary to popular belief, soft-shell crabs are not a variety of their own. They are blue crabs that have shed their hard shells in late spring in preparation for new ones. Soft-shell crabs are very delicate. They should not be deep-fried or overcooked. Be careful when you sauté them, as they tend to splatter badly. Your fish man will generally clean them for you, meaning he removes the head and the spongy substance, or soft gills, on each side of the body.

12 soft-shell crabs, cleaned

    Fresh lemon juice

3 tablespoons all-purpose flour

    Salt and pepper to taste

4 tablespoons butter

2 tablespoons vegetable oil

1 bunch scallions, thinly sliced

½ cup dry white wine

2 tablespoons parsley, finely chopped

Sprinkle the crabs with lemon juice and let them sit for a few minutes. Mix the flour, salt and pepper, and coat the crabs with it. Shake off excess flour. Heat butter and oil in a heavy sautéing pan, add the crabs and sauté them for 3 minutes with the top side down. Then turn them over and sauté for another 3 minutes. Remove crabs and keep warm. Add sliced scallions to the sautéing pan and sauté for a few minutes without letting them brown, then add wine and simmer for 3 minutes. Return crabs to the pan and reheat. Arrange the crabs on a preheated serving dish, pour the sauce over them and sprinkle with parsley.

Yield: 4 to 6 servings

Shrimp in Mustard Sauce

This makes a delicious cold dish, either as a first course, lunch or an after-theater supper, provided you can still afford the shrimp. Everybody generally loves it. Serve shrimp on a large platter or on individual plates on top of some lettuce leaves and decorated with a tomato rose and a sprig of parsley.

3   sprigs dill

1   onion, cut into quarters

4   cups water

2   pounds large shrimp (about 20 to 26 per pound), shelled and deveined

¼   cup finely chopped parsley

¼   cup finely chopped shallots

½   cup cider vinegar

½   cup light olive oil

2   tablespoons mustard (Grey Poupon or Pommery)

2   tablespoons chopped pimientos

Add the dill and onion to the water in a saucepan and bring it to a boil, simmering for 5 minutes. Then add the cleaned shrimp, keep on low heat until water again returns to a boil. Turn off the heat and let the shrimp sit in the water for about 2 minutes. Then take out the shrimp, discarding the dill and onion. (Don't throw out the liquid, though. Cool and freeze it. It will do as a fish stock when you are in a hurry or when you make your next shrimp sauce.) Put the shrimp into a bowl, combine the rest of the ingredients well and pour this sauce over the hot shrimp. Cover and marinate in your refrigerator for at least 1 hour before serving as described above.

Yield: 4 to 6 servings

Curried Shrimp

Although it is definitely not "real Indian" to serve any condiments other than chutney with curry, it can make your party very interesting and festive if you have more. Get a lot of pretty little bowls and fill them with some of these: sliced bananas, seedless grapes, kumquats, mandarin-orange slices, grated coconut, raisins, almonds, pecans, peanuts, chopped green or red pepper, chopped cucumber, chopped hard-boiled eggs, chopped bacon bits, etc.

2   tablespoons vegetable oil

2   yellow onions, chopped

1   green pepper, cleaned and chopped

    Salt and pepper to taste

    Dash of cayenne pepper, optional

1½   tablespoons curry powder

2   tablespoons all-purpose flour

1   10½-ounce can chicken broth, double strength

1   can water

½   cup white seedless raisins

2   pounds whole raw shrimp, cleaned

Heat vegetable oil in a heavy sautéing pan, add the onions and brown them lightly, then add the green pepper. Continue to sauté another 2 minutes, then add salt and pepper, cayenne, curry powder and flour. Combine all ingredients well, then add chicken broth, water and raisins. Bring to a boil and simmer over low heat for about 30 minutes. Now add shrimp, keep the heat low and simmer for another 3 minutes or until the shrimp are pink.

Yield: 4 servings

Vegetables

You hear a lot of cooking snobs say that the fresh vegetables in this country do not compare to those in Europe. This is not so. I have visited enough farms, particularly in the great state of New Jersey, to know that just the opposite is true. There is one difference however; when you visit a fruit and vegetable market in Europe, everything looks better. And that is because European women won't spend their money unless the greengrocer is putting out his best. I love farmers' markets, but finding one is no guarantee of fresh ingredients. Your best guide, of course, is your own judgment, and as we go along, I will give you ideas and tips on how to select fresh vegetables.

Stir-Fried Broccoli with Sesame Seeds

1   *bunch broccoli*

2   *tablespoons vegetable oil*

    Salt and pepper to taste

¼   *cup water*

¼   *cup sesame seeds*

1   *tablespoon sesame oil (Chinese)*

Wash the broccoli, cut off the flowerettes, peel the stems and cut them into thin diagonal slices. In a heavy sautéing pan, heat the oil. When it is very hot, add the broccoli, stirring constantly with a large spoon. Season with salt and pepper. Then add the water, cover and cook about 3 minutes, shaking the pan occasionally. Then add the sesame seeds and sesame oil, combine well and serve.

Yield: 4 servings

Stir-Fried Asparagus

2   *tablespoons vegetable oil*

1   *pound asparagus, washed, peeled and bottoms cut off stalks*

Cut the asparagus stalks diagonally into 2-inch pieces. In a heavy sautéing pan, heat the oil until it is very hot, add the asparagus, Spike, salt and pepper, and stir constantly. Cook for 1 minute. Then add the water, cover the pan immediately and cook for another 2 to 3 minutes, depending on the thickness of the stalks, shaking the pan occasionally.

Yield: 4 servings

½   tablespoon Spike
    seasoning

    Salt and pepper to
    taste

¼   cup water

Note: The only other method I use for cooking asparagus is steaming. Again, make sure not to overcook it.

Stir-Fried Vegetable Platter

The combinations of vegetables that can be stir-fried together are limitless. The stir-fry method has many virtues. It saves energy: yours and the stove's. It retains vitamins and minerals, but most important, the food tastes better. Make sure all your vegetables are cut in uniformly thin slices since the cooking time is so short.

2   tablespoons vegetable
    oil

3   stalks celery, washed
    and cut diagonally
    into slices

2   zucchini, washed, cut
    in half crosswise and
    cut into strips or slices

½   tablespoon Spike
    seasoning

½   pound snowpeas,
    washed and ends
    snipped off

1   pound bean sprouts,
    washed and dried

    Salt and pepper to
    taste

½   cup chicken broth,
    double strength, mixed
    with

1   tablespoon soy sauce
    and

1   teaspoon cornstarch

1   tablespoon chopped
    fresh parsley

In a heavy sautéing pan, heat oil. When very hot, add celery, zucchini, Spike, salt and pepper. Stir constantly for 1 minute. Add the snowpeas and stir another minute, then add the bean sprouts and cook another minute. Add the chicken broth, soy sauce and cornstarch mixture. Combine and let come to a boil. Remove from heat. Serve vegetables sprinkled with parsley.

Yield: 4 to 6 servings
Follow the same method with these vegetable combinations:

Celery, carrots and green beans
Zucchini, green peppers and red peppers
Parsnips, carrots and leeks
Snowpeas, mushrooms and bean sprouts

Tomato Fondue

The only time I make this recipe is when tomatoes are in season, which in my case means when the New Jersey beefsteak tomatoes are in. I used to serve it to Mrs. Kennedy whenever she had sautéed bay scallops. It also makes a great filling for omelettes and goes well with almost all fish dishes. I only use fresh basil with this since it is in season the same time the tomatoes are in season.

6   large tomatoes, peeled

2   tablespoons butter

1   tablespoon olive oil

2   tablespoons chopped shallots

1   tablespoon finely chopped fresh basil

Salt and pepper to taste

Cut the peeled tomatoes into quarters and remove the seeds, then cut into thin strips. Heat the butter and olive oil in a heavy sautéing pan, add the shallots and basil and sauté both lightly without browning them for about 2 minutes. Then add the tomato strips, season with salt and pepper and stir gently over low heat for about 2 minutes. Serve on a preheated platter and decorate with some fresh basil.

Yield: 4 to 6 servings

Note: To peel tomatoes, either put them into a saucepan with boiling water for 20 seconds, or if you only have 1 or 2 and cook with gas, spear them on a fork and rotate them over the flame until the skin blisters. Take a paring knife and simply peel off the skin.

Belgian Endives with Ham and Mornay Sauce

This is a most elegant vegetable dish that can also be served as a first course to a very elegant meal or as a luncheon dish along with a green salad. Belgian endives should be firm, closed, and white with yellow tips on the ends of the leaves when you buy them. They are grown in dark cellars and should not be stored in light, as the tips will turn green. There is another type of endive that is curly, and in fact, a lettuce. It is called chicory. Both names are used interchangeably in different locations, but you definitely want Belgian endives for this recipe. They have a slightly bitter taste that is very pleasant, but you should remove the hard core on the bottom because this part is too bitter. This is easily done with a small paring knife. Keep the endives refrigerated in plastic bags until ready to use. Pick out big plump ones for this dish or serve two per person.

6   large Belgian endives (or 12 small ones)

1   10½-ounce can chicken broth, double strength

Juice of 1 lemon

6   slices boiled ham or 6 slices prosciutto

Preheat broiler. Trim and wash the endives; cut off the bottom part. Use a skillet or sautéing pan that will comfortably hold all the endives. Pour the chicken broth and lemon juice over them, turn on the heat and bring to a boil; then reduce the heat to a gentle simmer. Cover the pan and braise the endives for 15 to 20 minutes until tender but still firm. Check this with a paring knife. It should go in fairly easily but still meet a little resistance.

Butter an ovenproof dish, preferably oval shaped. Wrap a slice of ham around each endive and put into the buttered dish.

Mornay Sauce:

4   *tablespoons butter*

4   *tablespoons all-purpose flour*

1   *cup of liquid in which you cooked endives*

1   *cup heavy cream*

½   *cup Parmesan cheese, grated*

½   *cup Switzerland Swiss cheese, grated*

Now make the sauce. Melt butter in a heavy saucepan, add the flour and cook this roux, stirring constantly, without letting it brown for 1 minute. Then add the cup of cooking liquid and the cream, stir with a whisk until sauce comes to a boil. Slowly stir in the grated cheeses. Pour this sauce over your ham-wrapped endives and put them under the preheated broiler until sauce is lightly browned and bubbly.

Yield: 6 servings

Green Beans with Shallots

Not long ago, one of the large food conglomerates did a test to determine whether or not our young people preferred real flavors to artificial flavors. I'm sure the results won't surprise you; they overwhelmingly preferred artificial flavoring because that's what they're used to. I'm sure you could try the same kind of test on most Americans with overcooked green beans and get the same kind of results because they have never had any other kind. I'd like you to walk into a field of fresh green beans some time, pick one and take a bite of it. Then ask yourself just how much more you need to do to it.

Whether or not you add shallots to your green beans, always cook them this way. Who knows, even your children might start to eat their vegetables and like them.

2   *pounds fresh green beans, washed, ends snipped, and cut in half*

2   *tablespoons vegetable oil*

3   *tablespoons chopped shallots*

½   *tablespoon Spike seasoning*

    Salt and pepper to taste

¼   *cup water*

After preparing the beans, put them into the refrigerator in a plastic bag to stay crisp until cooking time. If you are cooking them immediately, drop into a bowl of ice water as you cut them. Then drain in a colander.

In a heavy sautéing pan, heat the oil, add shallots and sauté until lightly browned. Add green beans, Spike, salt and pepper, and cook for 2 minutes, stirring constantly. Add water, cover and cook another 2 minutes, shaking the pan occasionally. Serve.

Yield: 6 servings

Flageolet Beans Provençale

Since the time I first made this dish for Mrs. Kennedy, I have learned to make it so it doesn't look, as she said, "like Boston Baked Beans." But then, sixteen years have gone by, and sometimes I wish I could make her just one more incredible feast to show her how she has inspired me.

If you cannot find flageolet beans, which are dried and imported from France, you can use dried lima beans instead. Make sure to soak them overnight, checking first for any impurities, like little stones. The beans can be cooked ahead of time and reheated, but add the tomatoes at the time of reheating so they retain their shape and don't turn mushy.

1 pound dried flageolet or baby lima beans, soaked overnight and drained

2 slices smoked bacon, cut into thin strips crosswise

1 yellow onion, chopped

1 clove garlic, put through garlic press

1 tablespoon thyme

1 bay leaf

2 10½-ounce cans chicken broth, double strength

Salt and pepper to taste

1 pound tomatoes, peeled, seeded and cut into thin strips or

1 -pound can of tomatoes, seeded and cut into thin strips

2 tablespoons chopped fresh parsley

Sauté the bacon in a heavy sautéing pan, add onion and sauté until very lightly browned. Then add garlic and thyme and sauté for another ½ minute. Add drained beans, bay leaf and chicken broth; if the broth does not completely cover the beans, add some water until it does. Bring to a boil, then turn down the heat to a low simmer. Cover pan and continue simmering for about 1 hour and 30 minutes. Then add salt and pepper as well as the tomato strips. Simmer for another 5 minutes and serve on preheated platter with parsley sprinkled on top.

Yield: 4 to 6 servings

Duchess Potatoes

Make sure that you use only cooking potatoes for this because baking potatoes have too mealy a texture. You can pipe the potatoes through a pastry bag fitted with an open star tube, either creating your own design in a buttered ovenproof dish, or making individual high rosettes on a buttered cookie sheet. After heating, remove rosettes with a spatula and put them around the lamb or whatever meat you're serving.

You can prepare the potatoes completely ahead of time. Just make sure you pour a little melted butter over them to prevent them from drying out in the reheating process. Keep in the refrigerator covered with plastic wrap supported by toothpicks stuck in the tops of the rosettes to avoid spoiling the shape of the potatoes.

6 medium-size cooking potatoes	Peel potatoes and cut into quarters. Steam them over water until soft but still firm. Put through a potato ricer or food mill. Whip the potatoes with an electric mixer, then add 1 teaspoon salt, the pepper and nutmeg. Beat whole eggs and yolks together until light and foamy and add to potatoes. Whip until fluffy. Put through a pastry bag as desired and bake in a preheated 450° F. oven until lightly browned.
1 teaspoon salt	
Pepper	
¼ teaspoon ground nutmeg	
2 whole eggs	
2 egg yolks	

Yield: 6 servings

Sautéed Potatoes with Garlic and Thyme

Contrary to popular belief, potatoes are not fattening. It's what you put on them that makes them fattening. When buying any potatoes, look for ones that are smooth, clean, fairly well shaped, uncut, unbruised and without sprouts.

2 tablespoons olive oil	In a heavy sautéing pan, heat the oil and butter. Then add the garlic and thyme and sauté for 30 seconds. Add the potatoes (if you soaked them in water, drain and dry on paper towels), salt and pepper, and cover. Cook over low heat for about 7 minutes, then turn the potatoes with a spatula, re-cover and cook another 7 minutes. Remove cover, turn potatoes again and continue cooking uncovered until they are nicely browned on all sides. Sprinkle with parsley and serve.
2 tablespoons butter	
2 cloves garlic, peeled and finely chopped	
1 tablespoon thyme	
2 pounds cooking potatoes, peeled and cut into ¼-inch slices (Keep in cold water until ready to use. This will prevent them from turning brown.)	
Salt and pepper to taste	
2 tablespoons chopped fresh parsley	

Yield: 4 to 6 servings

Baked Potatoes Stuffed with Cheese

One of the fondest memories of my childhood is potato-harvest time. After the fields were stripped clean, we would dig into the ground and find some potatoes that were overlooked. Then we built a fire with leaves and sticks in a pit, threw the potatoes on top of the hot coals, covered them with dirt and waited about an hour. Those potatoes emerged burned and dirty, but boy, were they good! And every fall when the weather turns cold, I get a great craving for a baked potato.

Don't bake potatoes in aluminum foil. If you want a steamed potato, it's easier to do it in your steamer. Scrub the baking potatoes well because the crisp, crunchy skin is the best part, and you don't want to eat the dirt. We've all outgrown that. It's okay to put metal skewers into the potatoes lengthwise; they will conduct the heat to the center and shorten the cooking time.

6 *baking potatoes*	
4 *tablespoons butter*	
1 *cup grated extra sharp Cheddar cheese*	
2 *eggs, beaten well*	
Dash of nutmeg	
Salt and pepper to taste	

Bake your potatoes in a 375° to 400° F. oven for about 1 hour. The time depends upon the size of your potatoes. When they are done, remove from the oven and cool a little, then cut lengthwise into halves and scoop out the potato meat, making sure to keep the skin intact. Put the potato meat into a bowl and break it up with a fork, then add the rest of the ingredients, mixing until all ingredients are well combined. Then take a spoon and refill the potato shells. Put them on a cookie sheet and reheat in a 400° F. oven for about 10 minutes.

Yield: 6 servings

Baked Potatoes with Sour Cream and Chives

6 *baking potatoes*	
3 *tablespoons butter*	
1 *cup sour cream*	
4 *tablespoons chopped fresh chives*	

Follow the same procedure as for the Baked Potatoes Stuffed with Cheese.

Yield: 6 servings

Note: How about putting a poached egg inside the shell and surrounding it with the potato mixture. Serve with a green salad, and you have a lunch that's terrific. Make the poached eggs in the morning and keep them refrigerated until ready to use. Otherwise, they will be turned into hard-boiled eggs in the reheating process.

Herbed Rice

This is a wonderful rice dish that goes well with lots of main courses. The addition of the herbs gives it a great taste.

2   tablespoons vegetable oil

3   scallions, cleaned and chopped

2   tablespoons parsley, chopped

2   tablespoons dill, chopped

1   teaspoon thyme

1   cup rice

1   10½-ounce can chicken broth, double strength

1   can water

Heat the vegetable oil in a saucepan, add the scallions and sauté them for a few minutes without letting them brown, then add the rest of the ingredients and combine well; bring to a boil and simmer for 20 minutes on low heat with the cover on. Turn off the heat and let rice stand for another 5 minutes.

Yield: 4 to 6 servings

Salads

During the summer months, lunch at the Cookingschool consists of salad because I want to enjoy the taste of really fresh greens and vegetables every chance I get. It is only during those months that we here in New York can enjoy that privilege. Any of you who live near a farm or grew up on one know the pure joy of eating freshly picked produce.

When you buy salad greens, do take care to wash them thoroughly. There is nothing worse than biting into gritty dirt. This is particularly true of spinach, which hides grains of sand very well. The next thing to remember is that a salad should, and always can, look appetizing. And probably the most important item is your salad dressing. How anyone can go to the trouble of washing lettuce and cutting up vegetables and then put bottled dressing on it is beyond me. Especially when making a good dressing is such an easy task.

I have experimented with all sorts of vinegars but have happily settled for plain old cider vinegar in my dressings. Salad oils are a more interesting and adventurous matter. I generally use a light-flavored oil, such as corn oil, safflower or sunflower, as a base. Then I add a small amount of more flavorful oil, such as walnut oil, hazelnut oil or sesame oil, depending on the salad. If you buy oil in a can, make sure you transfer it to a glass container once it is opened. It will stay fresher that way.

When it comes to mustard, I prefer Pommery mustard with its crushed mustard seeds and delicate flavoring. Also, Grey Poupon Dijon mustard, but save that for the hot dogs. The addition of herbs also perks up a salad; parsley is a must. Fresh dill is superb, fresh chives sublime and fresh tarragon, the ultimate. And what would a sliced fresh Jersey beefsteak tomato be without fresh basil?

Onions are another important flavor ingredient that should not be overlooked—thinly sliced scallions or green onions, Bermuda or Spanish onions, red Italian onions. One of my students from North Carolina sends me Valdeya onions. She says they're so sweet you can bite into them and they won't bite back. Fresh shallots are another treat, and what would a Caesar salad be like without garlic? Just romaine lettuce, I suppose. I could ramble on like this for quite a while, but I guess the best thing is just to put down some recipes.

One more thing: make sure to cut or tear lettuce to a size that is comfortable to eat with just a fork. There is nothing worse than having to maneuver large pieces of lettuce without a knife to cut them.

Summer Salad

This is the basic salad I serve as a main course. You may substitute any choice of other greens for the iceberg and romaine. I usually add either tuna or chicken, and sometimes thinly sliced beef, hard-boiled egg, radishes, black olives or any fresh crunchy vegetable that comes my way.

1   bunch watercress, large stems removed

1   head iceberg lettuce, cut into thin strips

1   small head romaine lettuce, cut into bite-size pieces

2   small cucumbers— gherkin, pickling, or Kirby—peeled and sliced

2   medium-size tomatoes, cut into eighths or 1 pint cherry tomatoes

Dressing:

½   cup vegetable oil

2   tablespoons olive oil

3   tablespoons cider vinegar

1   teaspoon honey

1   clove garlic, put through garlic press

½   cup grated Parmesan cheese

Put all dressing ingredients into a blender and mix until well combined.

You can either put all your greens into a bowl, pour the dressing over them, and toss, or you can arrange the salad ingredients decoratively on a platter, pour some of the dressing over them and serve the balance of the dressing on the side. In either case, serve with a bowl of extra grated Parmesan cheese and freshly ground pepper on the side.

Yield: 8 servings

Avocado, Orange and Romaine Salad

This makes a very pretty first-course salad. If you want it as a main course, you can add some cooked chicken cut into strips or chunks of cooked crab meat.

1 avocado, peeled and cut into thin slices

2 oranges, peeled and cut into thin slices

1 red onion, peeled and cut into thin slices

1 head of romaine lettuce, washed

Fresh lemon juice

Dressing:

½ cup vegetable oil

2 tablespoons walnut oil

3 tablespoons cider vinegar

1 teaspoon honey

1 tablespoon soy sauce

½ teaspoon grated ginger, optional

½ cup walnuts, coarsely chopped

Arrange the salad ingredients attractively on a platter. Sprinkle the avocado slices with some lemon juice to prevent them from turning dark.

Put all ingredients for the dressing except the nuts into a blender and blend well. Put into a bowl and add the nuts. Serve the dressing on the side.

Yield: 4 to 6 servings

Bean Sprout Salad

There used to be a time when I grew my own bean sprouts, but they are now so widely available that I find it unnecessary. When buying them, make sure they are white, not brown, and crispy to the touch. Keep in an open container of water in your refrigerator until ready to use, but generally for not more than 1 day. If you cannot find fresh ones, they now come in cans.

1 pound bean sprouts

2 cups boiling water

4 scallions or green onions, finely chopped

Put the fresh bean sprouts in a colander and pour the boiling water over them. Drain and put into a bowl. Add the rest of ingredients and mix well. Marinate for several hours in refrigerator before serving.

Yield: 4 servings

1 red pepper, cleaned
   and finely chopped

¼ cup vegetable oil

1 tablespoon sesame oil
   (Chinese)

1 tablespoon soy sauce

1 tablespoon cider
   vinegar

1 teaspoon honey

Potato and Cucumber Salad

This is really my version of German hot potato salad. In Germany, potato salads are very popular and are always served at room temperature, not really hot, and never refrigerated. Whatever kind of potato salad you make, I caution you that potatoes will not absorb dressing when cold, so always add your dressing soon after the potatoes are cooked. It is also important to use small cooking potatoes. They hold their shape much better. Never use baking potatoes for salad because they will fall apart. Try to find the long seedless cucumbers or small cukes.

3 pounds small potatoes

1 large seedless cucumber
   or 3 small cukes

½ Bermuda onion, finely
   chopped

1 dill pickle

4 tablespoons chopped
   parsley

Dressing:

¾ cup vegetable oil

2 tablespoons Dijon-style
   or Pommery mustard

4 tablespoons cider
   vinegar

   Salt and pepper to
   taste

Steam the potatoes in their skins. Pierce with a sharp knife to check doneness so that you don't overcook them. Remember, they will continue to cook in the skin for awhile after you remove them from heat. While potatoes are cooling, peel and thinly slice the cucumber, chop the onion and pickle. When potatoes are cool enough to handle, peel and slice them. Combine with cucumber, onion and pickle.

Put dressing ingredients in a blender and mix thoroughly. Pour this dressing over your salad and toss well. Cover and store at room temperature. Before serving, taste and add more vinegar if necessary. Sprinkle with chopped parsley.

Yield: 4 to 6 servings

Shrimp Salad with Avocado

4 cups water, approximately

1 tablespoon pickling spice

1 pound raw shrimp in the shell

1 large seedless cucumber or 3 pickling cucumbers, peeled and cut into cubes

4 stalks celery, chopped

1 avocado

Fresh lemon juice

Fresh parsley

Dressing:

½ cup mayonnaise

¼ cup catsup

1 tablespoon lemon juice

1 tablespoon chopped fresh dill

Put the water in a saucepan, add the pickling spice and bring to a boil, simmering for 5 minutes. Then add the shrimp and wait until water comes to a boil again, then turn off the heat. (With this cooking method, you will never get rubbery, hard shrimp.) Leave the shrimp in water for another 5 minutes, then take out, remove the shells, and devein if necessary.

Combine ingredients for dressing. Put shrimp into a bowl along with the cucumbers and celery, pour the dressing over them and toss well. Keep in the refrigerator until serving time.

Cut the avocado in half, peel and cut into thin slices, arranging them around your serving platter. Sprinkle with a little lemon juice to prevent from turning brown. Put shrimp salad in the middle and decorate with fresh parsley.

Yield: 4 to 6 servings

Asparagus Vinaigrette

This may surprise you. I am sure it would surprise a lot of restaurants, but fresh asparagus should always be peeled before cooking. The outer skin is stringy and bitter. Simply take a vegetable peeler and peel down from about 1 inch below the head, then cut off the fibrous end. I find that steaming asparagus is the best way to cook it because there is less danger of overcooking. The cooking time, once your water is boiling, will be anywhere from 2 to 5 minutes, depending on the thickness of the stalks. Check with a knife point; stalks should be slightly resistant when done. In this instance, since the asparagus is being served cold, immediately plunge it into ice water to stop the cooking. Do not put the vinaigrette dressing over spears until serving time, otherwise the asparagus will discolor.

2 pounds asparagus, cooked

Put the oils, vinegar, honey and mustard into a blender and blend well. Then put into a bowl, add eggs, parsley and pimiento, and combine well with a fork. Keep dressing refrigerated until ready to use.

Yield: 4 to 6 servings

Dressing:

- ½ cup vegetable oil
- 2 tablespoons olive or walnut oil
- 3 tablespoons cider vinegar
- 1 teaspoon honey
- 1 tablespoon Dijon-style or Pommery mustard
- 2 hard-boiled eggs, put through a coarse strainer
- 2 tablespoons finely chopped parsley
- 2 tablespoons finely chopped pimiento

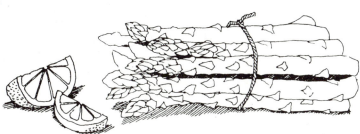

Asparagus and Chicken Salad

- 1 tablespoon sesame oil
- 2 pounds asparagus, peeled and cut diagonally into 1-inch pieces
- ½ teaspoon Spike seasoning

  Salt and pepper to taste

- 2 tablespoons soy sauce, mixed with
- ¼ cup chicken broth, double strength
- 2 cups cooked chicken, cut into thin strips
- 2 tablespoons cider vinegar

Heat the oil in a heavy sautéing pan or wok. When very hot, add the asparagus and stir-fry for 2 minutes, moving constantly with a large spoon. Add the Spike and salt and pepper, continue to stir another 30 seconds, add soy sauce and chicken broth, cover and cook 1 more minute. Turn off the heat, add the chicken and combine. Put on a platter and refrigerate until serving time. Just before serving, add vinegar and toss.

Yield: 4 to 6 servings

Spinach Mimosa Salad

Spinach salad is always a great favorite with almost everyone, and the variations on it are unlimited. Whenever you put hard-boiled egg yolks through a strainer into a salad, it is called mimosa. This is how this particular recipe gets its name.

1½   *pounds fresh spinach, washed and dried*

2   *hard-boiled egg yolks*

Dressing:

½   *cup vegetable oil*

2   *tablespoons olive oil*

2   *tablespoons cider vinegar*

2   *tablespoons Grey Poupon Dijon mustard*

1   *teaspoon honey*

Put dressing ingredients in a blender and blend for 60 seconds.

Put spinach in a bowl and pour dressing over it, toss salad well, making sure that all of the spinach is coated with the dressing. Then put the hard-boiled egg yolks through a coarse strainer and sprinkle over spinach salad.

Yield: 4 to 6 servings

Here are some additional variations on spinach salad:

Spinach and Mushroom.

Add to the spinach sliced fresh mushrooms and sprinkle some cooked and crumbled bacon over it. Use same dressing as above.

Spinach Salad Chinese Style.

Add to the spinach 2 cups of fresh bean sprouts and 2 hard-boiled eggs coarsely chopped. For the dressing, eliminate the mustard and add instead 2 tablespoons soy sauce.

Spinach and Chicken Salad.

Add to the spinach 2 cups of cooked chicken meat cut into strips or cubes; add 1 red pepper, washed, seeded and cut into strips or cubes. Serve with the following dressing. You may also sprinkle a few walnuts or pecans, coarsely chopped, over it.

½   *cup vegetable oil*

2   *tablespoons mayonnaise*

2   *tablespoons cider vinegar*

1   *tablespoon curry powder*

1   *teaspoon honey*

Put all dressing ingredients into a blender and blend until well combined.

Yield: 4 to 6 servings

Curried Chicken Salad

This salad makes a wonderful luncheon or a great addition to a summer buffet. Served on a bed of romaine lettuce, it looks even prettier.

1   *roasting chicken, poached, cooled, skinned and taken off the bone* or *about 4 cups of boneless chicken*

2   *Granny Smith apples, peeled and cored, cut into quarters and sliced crosswise*

1   *cup pecans, lightly broken*

1   *can pineapple chunks in their own juice, drained*

Dressing:

½   *cup mayonnaise*

¼   *cup vegetable oil*

1   *tablespoon curry powder*

1   *tablespoon chutney*

2   *tablespoons cider vinegar*

Put all dressing ingredients into your blender and blend until well combined. Put chicken, apples, pecans and pineapple into a bowl. Pour the dressing over them and mix well. Keep refrigerated for 30 minutes. Put the salad on romaine leaves and decorate with parsley and tomato roses.

Yield: 6 servings

Dilled Cucumber Salad

This is a wonderful all-purpose salad that I always serve with a cold salmon or striped bass, among other things. When buying cucumbers, try to find the long seedless ones called "gourmet" or "burpless." They are much more flavorful and have no seeds to remove. My second choice would be the small cukes referred to as pickling, gherkin or Kirby cucumbers. My last choice would be regular cucumbers, because these days they are heavily waxed for longer shelf life and have many seeds, which incidentally are completely indigestible. In any case, I suggest you always peel cucumbers because the skin is also indigestible. After peeling, cut off each end and taste a slice. If it tastes bitter, continue cutting and tasting slices until they no longer have a bitter taste. After making your salad, let it marinate for at least 30 minutes and taste again before serving. Cucumbers shed a lot of water, so you may have to pour off some of the dressing and add a little more vinegar. Dill I consider the perfect herb with cucumbers.

3   *cucumbers, thinly sliced*

½   *cup vegetable oil*

3   *tablespoons cider vinegar*

1   *tablespoon sugar or ½ tablespoon honey*

3   *tablespoons fresh dill, finely chopped*

Salt and pepper to taste

Peel the cucumbers, cut in half lengthwise and remove all seeds with a teaspoon. Slice the cucumbers very thinly and put in a bowl. Add the rest of the ingredients and combine well. Chill and keep refrigerated until serving time.

Yield: 6 servings

Gazpacho Salad

1   *head romaine lettuce, washed and dried*

3   *tomatoes, cut into cubes*

4   *pickling cucumbers, peeled and cut into cubes*

3   *green peppers, cleaned and cut into cubes*

3   *bunches scallions, cleaned and thinly sliced*

Dressing:

¼   *cup vegetable or olive oil, approximately*

3   *tablespoons cider vinegar*

    Salt and pepper to taste

Put the romaine lettuce leaves on a serving platter and arrange the tomatoes, cucumbers, peppers and scallions in a circle. Sprinkle vegetable or olive oil over salad, as well as the cider vinegar, and season with salt and pepper. Cover the salad with plastic wrap and marinate for about 20 minutes in the refrigerator before serving.

Yield: 4 to 6 servings

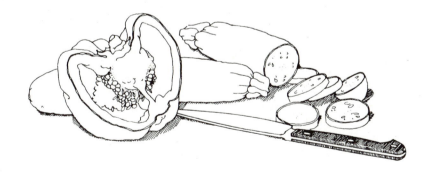

Baking

Baking is one area where it is very important that you understand why things work and, more important, why they don't, because nowhere else in cooking will your failures be more obvious. There was a time when baking was so much a part of family life that you just grew up knowing how to do it. You didn't think about why it worked, it just did. Today if you are a beginner it's pretty hard to find someone to teach you.

In this respect I was very lucky. No, I did not really learn to bake on the family hearth. It was many years later. My former partner decided to take a summer course in baking at The Culinary Institute in Hyde Park some years ago, and I decided to go along. At that time I was not a great baker, nor did I profess to be, but I certainly felt I knew most of the answers. Well, that was my first mistake.

Our first session was held in a small classroom, and while we waited for the instructor, introductions were made among the students, all of whom were professionals. Everybody recognized me, or my name, with the usual "Aren't you the girl, etc." You know the rest.

By the time the instructor arrived I was feeling pretty important. And when he did arrive we did not know he was the incomparable Albert Kumin, probably the greatest pastry chef in the world. Mr. Kumin proceeded to describe the things we were going to make that afternoon in the bakeshop, the first one being piecrust. As he listed the ingredients, I interrupted him very brightly with "Excuse me, sir, I always add a little lemon juice to my dough." Now Albert—I use that familiar name because we have since become great friends—is one of the kindest of all men, so instead of cutting off my head he simply said, "Ya, you can do dat but it will make your dough tough, no?"

I should have known right then to quit while I was only a little behind, but I didn't. "Also," I said, "you didn't mention unbleached flour. I always tell my students to use unbleached flour." Again, Albert, the soul of patience, replied: "How should I say—you can use unbleached flour for some things, but your yeast doughs don't rise so good, ya?" At this point Joe put his head into his hands and I nodded weakly and tried to disappear into the woodwork.

Those two weeks with Albert Kumin were a revelation to both of us. We learned so many things, and I will pass along all I have space for.

Flour is the most important ingredient in baking. Therefore, the quality of the flour you use will have a major influence on the quality of the product you turn out. By quality I do not mean the brand name, I mean the way it is made.

It is not important that you know all about the different kinds of flour used in a bakery, but I will describe them as a matter of interest. It is important, however, that whenever possible you use the right kind of flour. So I am going to give you some tips on how to improvise with the flour you can get.

Here are the basic flours you would find in a bakeshop. They are generally unavailable except through wholesalers in 100-pound bags, except for cake flour.

High-Gluten Flour:	Made from hard wheat and used for hard rolls and hearth breads.
Patent or *Bread Flour:*	Made from hard wheat and used in most breads and rolls.
Pastry or *Pie Flour:*	Made from soft wheat, high in starch, low in gluten and used in piecrust, cookies and pastry.
Cake Flour:	Made from soft wheat, high in starch, low in gluten and used for cakes, muffins and biscuits.

Now obviously, one flour is missing. *All-Purpose Flour.* All-purpose flour fits right in the middle. It is a combination of hard-wheat flour and soft-wheat flour. It is designed to give you a convenient flour that will do all the jobs of the other flours. Does it? Sure, it does a fair job, but not a great job.

Here are a couple of ways you can improve on your all-purpose flour.

If you cannot get cake flour, you can add cornstarch to your all-purpose flour to make it softer. In other words, you are increasing the proportion of starch to gluten in the flour for cakes. You want a flour high in starch and very low in gluten. Add ¼ cup of cornstarch to ¾ cup of all-purpose flour. For pie dough, add two cups cake flour to one cup all-purpose and sift together twice. This will give you a much finer pie dough and one that is easier to roll.

Here is my recipe for pie dough using pastry flour. It differs slightly from my recipes using all-purpose flour because here we are using 3 ounces of shortening and 3 ounces of butter rather than 6 ounces of butter.

Basic Pie Dough

2 *cups pastry flour (2 parts cake flour to 1 part all-purpose)*

3 *ounces butter (¾ stick)*

3 *ounces vegetable shortening*

⅓ *cup ice water*

The way you mix your pie dough is very important. It is not difficult; on the contrary, it is very simple.

Sift your flour together twice into a large bowl. If you have a heavy-duty mixer with a paddle attachment or dough hook, use mixer bowl. Or you may use a food processor.

Have your butter very cold, frozen if possible; cut the butter into cubes about the size of a cherry and add to the flour. Turn on the mixer to low speed or knead the butter into the flour very quickly with your fingertips. Do not break up the butter cubes too fine. You want to retain tiny lumps of butter.

Add the shortening and mix another 2 minutes. Slowly add as much of the ice water as needed. You should just be able to pat pastry into a ball. Mix quickly. Depending upon the weather, you may not need all the water. Do not overmix.

Cut the dough in half and shape it into discs. Wrap with plastic wrap or waxed paper and refrigerate for at least 12 hours; 24 hours, if possible. I will explain the reason later. All this may sound tedious to you, but remember, once you have mastered this very simple procedure, you will always turn out a dough for your pies, tarts or quiches that is as professional as anything made.

You are going to find that rolling this dough is easier than rolling dough made with all-purpose flour. The reason is simple; it has less gluten. It is a soft dough, and it is a relaxed dough because whatever gluten it contains has been resting in your refrigerator overnight. So the last thing you want to do now is stretch it too much or do anything to make it tough.

So take half the dough for the bottom of your pie or quiche and roll it so that the circle is about 2 inches wider than your pan on all sides.

You may roll your dough on a lightly floured board or a marble slab or between two pieces of waxed paper. Be careful not to use too much flour on either the surface or rolling pin. If you use waxed paper, turn the dough over several times as you roll it. This will give you a more even crust.

Do not roll pie dough bigger than you need it, because it cannot be rerolled. You may not believe this, but if you do roll it twice, it will look fine until you bake it; then it will shrink very disastrously. In an emergency, you can reroll the trimmings for the bottom of a pie that has a heavy filling, but the results are never very good.

When the dough is rolled to the proper size, drape it over your rolling pin and carefully ease it snugly into the bottom of the pan. Avoid stretching it. Trim it with a knife or scissors.

At this stage you can give yourself a little more insurance against shrinkage by putting the shell into the refrigerator or freezer to rest for 30 minutes or longer.

Note: I use shortening here because it will give you a flaky crust. Butter will not. On the other hand, shortening has no flavor and butter does. You may increase the proportion of shortening to butter if you like to get an even flakier crust, but you will sacrifice flavor. If you are curious, vegetable shortening is merely vegetable oil that is injected with hydrogen to make it solid.

If you wish to make a large quantity of pie dough, the proportions are always the same: 3 parts flour, 2 parts shortening, 1 part water. In other words, you could use 3 pounds of pastry flour, 2 pounds of butter and shortening and 1 pound of water (which is 1 pint).

This dough will freeze very well for many months if well wrapped.

Strawberry Tart with Crème Pâtissière

This is one of the most glorious desserts I know. And the recipe lends itself to any number of variations by simply substituting other fresh fruit for the strawberries, such as raspberries (if you can afford them), poached peaches, seedless grapes, cherries. Because it is such a versatile dessert, I am going to take some care explaining to you how to make it right.

Baked Pie or Tart Shell:

2   *cups pastry flour (2 parts cake flour to 1 part all-purpose)*

3   *ounces butter (¾ stick)*

3   *ounces vegetable shortening*

⅓   *cup ice water*

For this dessert and any other cold tart, you must bake your piecrust empty, which is called "blind." There are, I suppose, as many ways to do this as there are cookbooks. This is my favorite method: it's simple and fairly foolproof.

To bake a "blind" shell, roll out basic pie dough and line a 10-inch tart pan. Refrigerate for at least 30 minutes. Preheat oven to 375° F. Line the chilled shell snugly with a piece of aluminum foil. Fill the foil with raw rice and shake to make sure rice is evenly distributed. Bake in the middle rack of the 375° F. oven for 25 to 30 minutes. When the rim of the pastry is a nice light brown, remove from the oven. Remove foil and rice from the shell and put aside for future use.

At this point, brush the crust with some apricot jam. This will prevent the crust from becoming soggy when you have the crème pâtissière inside. Return the crust to the oven and continue baking for another 5 to 10 minutes until well browned all over. Set aside to cool.

Note: This is as good a time as any to impress upon you one fact. In order to be a successful baker, you must rely on your own senses; your eyes, your nose and your fingers, not a kitchen timer. You won't find a kitchen timer in many bakeries (unless they are waiting for the coffee break). In the first place, the chemistry of food is too complex and unpredictable; in the second place, ovens, particularly gas ovens, are notoriously fickle. True, you should always strive for correct oven temperatures by checking often with an oven thermometer and, when there is a large discrepancy, having it adjusted. But I have cooked with ovens that worked perfectly one day and were completely crazy the next; so you must learn to rely on your own judgment, not on the little bell. I always tell you what the right temperature and time should be, but also how the item should look or feel when baked properly.

Crème Pâtissière (Pastry Cream):

1 cup milk

3 egg yolks

⅓ cup sugar

½ teaspoon pure vanilla extract

¼ cup all-purpose flour

Bring the milk to a boil in a heavy saucepan and set aside. Put the egg yolks, sugar and vanilla into the bowl of an electric mixer and beat until light and fluffy. Add the flour and mix well. Then with the mixer at medium speed, slowly add the hot milk to the egg custard. Pour the custard back into the saucepan and stir constantly with a whisk over medium heat until it comes to a boil. Reduce the heat and stir another 2 minutes. Pour into a bowl and refrigerate until completely cooled.

Note: This very useful and delicious custard filling for pastries and cakes can be made in any flavor: vanilla, chocolate, lemon, etc.; you can add rum, brandy, liqueurs, etc.; you can add whipped cream to it to fill cream puffs. It is very similar to Vanilla Bavarian Cream, which we will discuss in the dessert chapter, except it is thicker. Because it contains flour, you can bring it to a boil without curdling the eggs. This recipe is very simple, but be careful to stir constantly to avoid scorching it.

Now you are ready to make the strawberry tart.

Strawberry Tart:

Crème pâtissière

1 pint fresh strawberries, washed, hulled and dried

½ cup red currant jelly

Remove the cooled tart shell from the pan and fill shell with the crème pâtissière. Place the whole strawberries on top in concentric circles, with point side up. Melt the currant jelly in a saucepan until it is liquid, then cool slightly until it is the consistency of egg whites. Using a small pastry brush, coat each strawberry with the currant glaze.

Yield: 1 10-inch tart

Tarte aux Poires aux Amandes

If you want to look like a superstar, this is the recipe that will do it. It was one of Mrs. Kennedy's favorites, and after you taste it you'll know why.

You can buy the almond paste in the "gourmet" section of some supermarkets or in specialty shops. The brands I have seen are imported from Denmark. For the garnish, you should buy shelled raw pistachio nuts. Blanch them in boiling water for 10 seconds and remove the skin.

Fill a 10-inch tart shell with Basic Pie Dough (see page 118). Refrigerate.

Filling:

1	*pound almond paste*
4	*whole eggs*
¼	*cup granulated sugar*
½	*pound sweet butter*
⅓	*cup cake flour*
½	*cup apricot preserves, melted and cooled*
¼	*cup chopped unsalted pistachios*
3	*poached pears, cut lengthwise in half, then cut crosswise into 4 slices and reassembled so that they look like halves*

Take the almond paste and 1 egg white (from the whole eggs) and the sugar and work the almond paste smooth in the bowl of an electric mixer. (The paste should be smooth, but never oily.) Then add the butter and mix well. Scrape your bowl and gradually add your eggs, scraping the bowl once or twice. Take the bowl from the mixer and fold in the flour. Mix well and spoon half of the frangipane cream (the almond-paste mixture) into the pastry shell. Bake the tart on the lower rack of a preheated 350° F. oven for about 20 minutes.

After the tart is baked and cooled, put the remaining frangipane cream into it. Then arrange the 6 reassembled pear halves on the cream like the spokes of a wheel, with the narrow ends of the pears facing the middle of the tart. Gently flatten and spread the slices so they reach the outer rim of the tart. Bake 15 minutes more and remove from oven.

When the tart is cooled, brush the top with the apricot glaze and sprinkle with chopped pistachios.

Yield: 1 10-inch tart

Caramel Glazed Apple Tart with Hazelnut Crust

Hazelnut Crust:

This dough is identical to the Basic Pie Dough (see page 118) with the addition of chopped hazelnuts (filberts). Simply add ½ cup finely chopped hazelnuts to the dough with the shortening and refrigerate overnight.

Roll out half the dough, reserving the other half for a later use, and fill a 10-inch tart pan. Refrigerate.

Filling:

4   *Granny Smith apples, peeled, cored, cut in half*

1   *cup sugar*

½   *cup apricot preserves*

Preheat oven to 350° F. Take each apple half and make the thinnest possible slices of uniform size. Place them in the tart shell in concentric circles, starting from the outside. Place one slice upon the next so that they almost completely overlap. You will have room for two large circles. Then arrange an attractive pattern to fill the middle.

Melt the sugar in a heavy saucepan over medium heat until it turns light caramel-colored, stirring occasionally. Then quickly pour the caramel over the apples in concentric circles. Put tart on the middle rack of your oven and bake for about 35 minutes, or until the shell is nicely browned.

While the tart is cooking, melt the apricot preserves in a saucepan, and cool slightly. After the tart is removed from the oven, but while it is still slightly warm, brush the top with apricot glaze.

Yield: 1 10-inch tart

Apple Pie with Cheddar Cheese Crust

This is Joe's recipe from The Great Take-Out, and although I am not an "American Apple-Pie Mom," I adore this one. I love it best when it is slightly warm and he pours a little heavy cream into the opening in the top. Sinful but so good.

The crust is the same as the Basic Pie Dough (see page 118) except the sugar is omitted and sharp Cheddar cheese added.

Cheddar Cheese Crust:

2   cups pastry flour (2 parts cake flour to 1 part all-purpose)

3   ounces cold unsalted butter

3   ounces vegetable shortening

1   cup grated sharp Cheddar cheese (3/4 cup in dough, 1/4 cup set aside)

1/2   teaspoon salt dissolved in

1/3   cup ice water

Prepare dough as in basic recipe. Add 3/4 cup Cheddar cheese with the shortening. Reserve the other 1/4 cup of cheese. Divide and refrigerate the dough exactly the same as the basic pie dough.

When you roll the dough, sprinkle the remaining 1/4 cup of cheese over the two discs before you roll them. Roll out your bottom crust and line your pie dish. Roll out top crust and place on a sheet of waxed paper. Refrigerate crusts for at least 30 minutes.

Filling:

3   tablespoons butter

7   Granny Smith apples, peeled, cored and sliced

1   tablespoon lemon juice

1   cup light brown sugar

1/8   teaspoon cinnamon

Dash of freshly ground nutmeg

1   tablespoon cornstarch mixed with

1/3   cup water or calvados (French apple brandy)

2   tablespoons cream mixed with

Preheat oven to 400° F. To make the filling, melt the butter in a heavy saucepan. Add 1/3 of the apples, the lemon juice, brown sugar, cinnamon and nutmeg. Cover and simmer over low heat for about 3 minutes. Add the cornstarch and water or calvados and simmer another minute. Add the remaining apples. Mix well and take off heat to cool completely.

Fill the pie shell with the apple mixture. Brush the rim of the shell with the egg wash. Cut a hole in the center of the pie top, about 3/4" in diameter, with a round pastry tube or knife. Fit the top on the pie and press the pastry together around the rim with a fork or crinkle it with your fingers. Brush the top with the remaining egg wash. Bake in the center of the oven for about 45 minutes, until the crust is a golden brown. Right before serving, pour 2 or 3 tablespoons of heavy cream into the hole in the crust.

Yield: 1 10-inch pie

1 egg yolk, to make egg
wash

2 or 3 tablespoons heavy
cream

Pecan Diamonds

Short Dough:

1   cup unsalted butter

¾   cup plus 2 tablespoons
granulated sugar

½   cup shortening
(Crisco)

2   eggs

5¼ cups all-purpose flour

½   teaspoon vanilla
extract

To make short dough, cream the butter, sugar and shortening until well combined and smooth. Then add the rest of the ingredients and mix until just combined. Do not overmix. Pat the pastry into a jelly-roll pan. Then prick the pastry all over with a fork and prebake in a 350° F. oven for 15 minutes. Cool in the pan, then put the pan into another jelly-roll pan. The reason for the second pan is to keep the bottom of the crust from overbaking.

Pecan Filling:

1   cup unsalted butter

1⅛   cups light brown
sugar

4   tablespoons
granulated sugar

½   cup honey

1   pound pecans (4
cups), coarsely
chopped

¼   cup heavy cream

In the meantime, put the butter, brown sugar, granulated sugar and honey in a saucepan and bring to a boil. Boil for 3 minutes. Do not stir during this time. Then take the mixture off the heat and add the pecans and heavy cream and combine well. Pour this filling into your prebaked crust and bake for 35 minutes in a 350° F. oven.

When pouring the filling, reserve a little to fill the corners, because this filling does not flow very well. After baking and cooling, cut in the pan into small squares or diamond shapes with a pizza cutter or serrated knife. Do not refrigerate before cutting or the caramel will be too hard to cut.

Yield: approximately 3 dozen

Baking Cakes

Although you may not be too excited about baking cakes, I feel that it is very important to know how to make one cake very well. Unless you do learn, your ability to make desserts will never be complete. In other words, you don't learn to bake a cake so you can whip up a birthday cake—although that is always nice to know how to do—but rather so you can make all the desserts that require some form of cake.

There are basically two kinds of cakes (I am ignoring angel food): butter cakes and sponge cakes. Butter cakes are more common in America than in Europe. When properly made, they are tender, rich and moist and are superb layer cakes. Sponge cakes are much lighter, less rich, but much more versatile. In fact, they are the base of almost all tortes in Europe. They are also much easier to make properly than butter cakes.

For the sake of information, butter cakes are made by creaming together butter and sugar, adding egg yolks and flavoring, then flour, baking powder, milk and finally folding in beaten egg whites. The baking powder provides most of the leavening, or rising ability; the egg whites the rest. Sponge cakes, on the other hand, generally contain only beaten eggs, sugar, flavoring and flour. The leavening is provided solely by the beaten eggs.

The one cake I would like you to master is the genoise. This is really a butter-sponge cake. Both the French and the Italians take credit for it; whoever created it (I'm sure it must be German), it is a wonderfully useful cake. With it you can make any kind of roll: jelly roll, lemon roll, chocolate roll. You can use it for layer cakes, sheet cakes, icebox cakes, strawberry shortcake. In other words, there is no limit to its uses.

The genoise is simply a basic sponge cake to which you add melted butter. This makes the sponge richer.

Here are the important points to remember about making a butter-sponge:

1. Make sure your mixer bowl and beaters are clean and free from grease or fat. Any fat will prevent your eggs from beating properly.
2. Measure your flour accurately. When recipes refer to a cup of sifted flour, it means a cup of flour after it has been sifted. Fill a stainless-steel 1-cup measure with flour and run a flat knife edge across the top to level it.
3. Your eggs must be beaten enough and the sugar completely dissolved in them.
4. Make sure the melted butter is completely cool. Otherwise your sponge might collapse.
5. Make sure your eggs are at room temperature. This will give you greater volume in the batter. You may warm the eggs and sugar over a hot water bath before beating them (make sure you don't cook the eggs). This will make your sponge even lighter and firmer.
6. Bake at correct temperature. Remember this rule: the higher the cake, the lower the temperature. So in this case, if you are using two 9-inch layer cake pans or one jelly-roll pan, you bake it at 375° F. If you are using one high 10-inch cake pan, you would drop the oven temperature 25° F. to 350° F. When you think the cake is done, press the top with your finger. When completely baked, and not before, the cake will spring right up again.
7. Sponge cakes freeze very well if they are carefully covered with a double layer of plastic wrap.

Genoise

This recipe differs from the "classic" genoise recipe you will find in a lot of books in two respects. One, it contains extra egg yolks, and two, it contains baking powder.

When Albert Kumin was in charge of the bakeshop at the World Trade Center, here in New York, I spent several days working there as an apprentice. And I can tell you it was quite an experience. They make all the bread, rolls, cakes, cookies, pastries, etc., for all the restaurants, including Windows on the World, and the retail bakeshops in those two enormous buildings. The amount of food they turn out every day is staggering. At any rate, Albert assigned me to help make layer cakes. After the butter-sponge cakes are baked and cooled, they are sliced horizontally into three layers. And this can mean several hundred cakes at any one time. I noticed that his cakes were less fragile than mine and therefore a lot easier to slice. He pointed out to me that "in the field" (in other words, the everyday life of a bakeshop), they added extra egg yolks to the sponge to give it more body. Although this is an added expense it pays off in time and labor savings.

The baking powder is my little insurance policy. Having made hundreds of these cakes, I know that sometimes they will collapse for no reason that I can figure out. To prevent that, I add ⅛ teaspoon baking powder. Nobody can tell it's there except the cake batter. It doesn't affect the taste at all, and it works.

5	whole eggs
3	egg yolks
1	cup sugar
¼	teaspoon pure vanilla extract
¾	cup all-purpose flour
¼	cup cornstarch
⅛	teaspoon baking powder

In a large mixing bowl, place the eggs, egg yolks, sugar and vanilla, and beat with the electric mixer until mixture forms ribbons. (It will turn pale yellow and be light and fluffy). In another bowl, combine the flour, cornstarch and baking powder and sift thoroughly. Add this mixture to your beaten eggs very gently but combine thoroughly.

Line the bottom of a 10-inch springform mold with parchment paper and butter the sides. Pour in the batter and bake in a preheated 350° F. oven for about 40 minutes. Cool the cake for a few minutes, then remove from the pan and cool on a cake rack.

Yield: 1 10-inch cake

Strawberry Cheese Torte

This is a cake you definitely must make for someone you love. In fact, it is my daughter's favorite. It has all the best features of a cheesecake and a strawberry shortcake. It is delicious and spectacular looking. The genoise cake can be made well in advance and frozen until ready to use.

1	*genoise cake, sliced horizontally into 3 layers*
2	*pints fresh strawberries, washed, hulled, cut in half and macerated with*
¼	*cup of sugar*
2	*tablespoons framboise (raspberry brandy), optional*
1	*package unflavored gelatin (Knox), dissolved in*
¼	*cup water*
1	*pound cream cheese, at room temperature*
¾	*cup granulated sugar*
1	*ounce brandy or cognac or 1 tablespoon of pure vanilla extract*
	Grated rind of 1 lemon
3	*cups heavy cream*

To layer your genoise, place on a counter close to the edge. Place one hand on top of the cake; with a long, serrate-edged knife, carefully cut the first of three layers from the bottom. Keep the knife level and cut one-third through the cake. Then slowly revolve the cake as you cut through the remaining two-thirds. (It is very important to remove the bottom layer and cut the next layer the same way. Don't be too upset if your layers don't come out perfectly the first few times. Just go ahead and use them because they will be covered with filling.) Put your best outside layer on the bottom of a 10-inch cake pan, because after unmolding, it will be the top of the cake.

Sprinkle strawberries with sugar and framboise and let them macerate for at least 10 minutes. Fill a 1-cup Pyrex measuring cup ¼ full of cold water. Sprinkle a package of unflavored gelatin into the water. Stir with a spoon and allow the gelatin to soften. Place the cup into a shallow pan of boiling water until the gelatin is completely liquid, then remove the cup from the pan and set aside to cool. Put the cream cheese in the bowl of an electric mixer and beat until smooth; add the ¾ cup sugar, brandy or vanilla, and lemon rind and continue beating until very light. Add the dissolved gelatin, mix well and remove bowl from mixer. In another bowl, whip the heavy cream, then fold into the cheese mixture. Reserve 2 cups of mixture for frosting the outside of the cake and some of the strawberries for decoration.

Pour some of the cheese-cream mixture over the first layer of genoise in the cake pan, smooth it and cover with strawberries. Add the second layer of cake, more cheese-cream mixture and strawberries, then the third and last layer of cake. Refrigerate the cake for at least 2 hours. When you are ready to unmold it, fill the sink with very hot water and place the cake pan in the water for 10 seconds. Place a serving platter over the pan and invert the cake to unmold. Frost the top and sides with the reserved cheese-cream mixture and decorate with strawberries and fresh mint leaves.

Yield: 1 10-inch torte

Note: Hulling strawberries is not the same as slicing off the tops. The green top is attached to a core inside the berry, both of which should be removed. In this way, you will retain the beautiful shape of the berry, have no waste, and get rid of the core, which has no flavor. Simply take a sharp paring knife and cut down at a sharp angle around the green top and pull out the core at the same time.

Chocolate Chocolate Cake

If you are a member of that ever-growing band of chocolate lovers, this cake should fulfill your wildest fantasies, and it is worth every calorie. It is a chocolate genoise baked with Swiss cocoa and bittersweet chocolate bits. Then it is layered with the most extravagantly rich chocolate canache cream, then covered and smothered with more. You can save yourself some time by picking your next diet before you start making it.

Chocolate Genoise:

5	whole eggs
3	egg yolks
1	cup sugar
¼	teaspoon vanilla extract
½	cup cake flour
½	cup Swiss cocoa powder
⅛	teaspoon baking powder
2	ounces grated bittersweet chocolate

Preheat oven to 350° F. Line the bottom of a 10-inch springform mold with parchment paper and butter the sides. In the bowl of an electric mixer, add the eggs, yolks, sugar and vanilla, and beat until it forms ribbons or until you can draw a ridge with your finger. Sift together the flour, cocoa and baking powder and fold into the batter, gently but thoroughly. Fold in the grated chocolate. Pour the batter into the prepared mold and bake for about 40 minutes or until the cake springs back to your touch. Cool the pan a few minutes, then unmold genoise and cool on a cake rack.

Canache Cream:

1	cup heavy cream
¼	cup sugar
2	ounces butter (½ stick)
1	pound (16 ounces) bittersweet or semisweet chocolate
1	ounce bittersweet chocolate for decoration

Put cream, sugar and butter into a saucepan and bring to a boil, stirring occasionally. Add the chocolate and stir until melted. Cool the mixture, then transfer to the bowl of an electric mixer and whip until light and fluffy.

Slice the chocolate genoise horizontally into three layers. Fill the layers and then frost the top and sides with the canache cream. Using a pastry bag and star tube, decorate the top with chocolate rosettes. Then with a vegetable peeler, shave 1 ounce chocolate over the rosettes.

Yield: 1 10-inch cake

Note: It is important to note that the best packaged chocolate comes from Switzerland. All chocolate is frightfully expensive these days, but the extra cost of Swiss is worth it; it will make a world of difference in your desserts. Droste and Van Houten I consider the finest cocoa. For bittersweet or milk chocolate, I recommend Tobler, Lindt, or Poulain, which has recently been imported from France.

Black Forest Torte

1   chocolate genoise

3   cups heavy cream

½   cup confectioners' sugar

1   package unflavored gelatin dissolved in

¼   cup water (see method on page 18)

1   cup basic syrup flavored with kirsch (see below)

3   cups pitted sour cherries marinated overnight in

¼   cup sugar and

3   tablespoons kirsch

1   small can pitted bing cherries and chocolate curls for decoration

Cut the chocolate genoise into three layers (as described in recipe for Strawberry Cheese Torte, page 127). Whip the heavy cream. As it starts to thicken, add the confectioners' sugar and then the dissolved gelatin and continue whipping until stiff. Put the bottom layer of cake on your serving platter and brush it with some of the basic kirsch syrup. Fit a pastry bag with a No. 5 star tube, fill with the whipped cream and pipe a ring around the outside of the layer and another around the inside. Then pipe another ring between the two. Arrange marinated sour cherries between the rings. Apply second layer, brush with syrup and follow same procedure. Place last layer on top and spread top and sides with whipped cream. Make sixteen rosettes around top edge of cake. Place a cherry on each and sprinkle chocolate shavings in center of cake.

Yield: 1 10-inch torte

Basic Syrup Flavored with Kirsch:

1   cup sugar

2   cups water

1   lemon cut into slices

½   orange cut into slices

¼   cup kirsch

Combine ingredients, except kirsch. Bring to a boil, stirring occasionally, then simmer for about 20 minutes. Strain and cool and add the kirsch. This syrup can be kept for several weeks in your refrigerator, stored in a glass jar. If you have ever wondered how professionals make their cakes so moist, this is the answer. You can flavor this syrup with any liqueur.

Yield: 3¼ cups syrup

Note: Next time you have some leftover whipped cream from decorating a dessert, put a sheet of waxed paper on a cookie sheet and pipe the rest of the cream into little stars on the paper. Freeze them for about 1 hour and put into a plastic container. It will save you from having to whip the cream next time you decorate a mousse, or pop them straight from the freezer into your coffee for Coffee mit Schlag, one of my favorites.

Cheesecake

New York City could be called the Cheesecake Capital of the World. There are very few restaurants or bakeries in this great city that do not serve cheesecake. I would prefer to call it "The Bad Cheesecake Capital." Frankly, I am at a complete loss to explain why it is so difficult to find a decent cheesecake in New York. Perhaps it is the vast competition to create something complicated out of something so simple. In any event, this recipe is not complicated. It is simple and superb.

2½	pounds cream cheese, at room temperature
1½	cups granulated sugar
7	eggs
4	egg yolks
1	teaspoon vanilla extract or grated rind of 1 lemon
½	cup heavy cream

Preheat oven to 400° F. Put the cream cheese into the bowl of an electric mixer and cream until very light. Then add the sugar and eggs and egg yolks, and cream well. Scrape down the sides of the bowl several times with a rubber spatula. Add the flavoring and beat well until the batter is smooth, then add the heavy cream and continue mixing. Butter a deep 9-inch cake pan (not a springform pan) and cover the bottom with a thin layer of baked sponge cake or a graham-cracker crust. Pour the batter into the cake pan. Put the cake pan into a larger baking pan. Place it on the middle rack of your oven and pour boiling water into the larger pan until it covers the bottom half of your cake pan. Stir the top of the batter with a spoon just before baking. Bake for about 1 hour. Cool in pan.

Yield: 1 9-inch cake

Graham Cracker Crust:

1½	cups graham-cracker crumbs (about 20 cracker squares)
⅓	cup butter, softened
½	cup sugar

Blend all ingredients together and press them into the bottom of your cake pan.

Here are some important hints:

1. Stirring the top of the batter just before baking will prevent the top of the cake from cracking.
2. Check the cake after 40 minutes. If the top is getting too brown, cover it with a piece of parchment paper or buttered aluminum foil.
3. After 1 hour, press the top of the cake with your finger. If surface springs right up again, the cake is done.
4. This cake must be cooled slowly in the pan. Put the pan on a cake rack so air will circulate under the bottom.
5. When the cake is cooled, invert onto a plate and then invert again onto another plate so it is right side up.
6. This is a very rich, creamy cake, so it is hard to cut with a knife. I suggest using a wire cake cutter, or simply take a long piece of very strong thread, wrap around the fingers of both hands, and press it down, cutting the cake in half, then in quarters, etc.

Fudge Brownies

Although all of my students have at one time or another gotten this recipe from me, I feel I'd like to share it with those who don't have it yet, since it is probably one of my most well-known recipes. I generally have an ample supply of these brownies in my freezer. (They're so fudgy, they have to be kept there.) And whenever I go to a business meeting, the wholesale flower market, my banker, or anyone else in whose grace and memory I want to stay, I bring a package of brownies wrapped up with ribbons and a fresh flower on top, so they look more like a gift from Tiffany's. And believe me, it works. I have managed to make the part of New York that's important to me my own little town, where you can hear, "Hey, Annemarie, didn't you bring some brownies?" It works even better than sex appeal.

2	sticks butter
9	ounces unsweetened chocolate (Baker's)
9	eggs
4½	cups sugar
1	teaspoon salt
1	tablespoon vanilla extract
2¼	cups all-purpose flour
1½	cups pecans

Preheat oven to 325° F. In a heavy sautéing pan, melt the butter, then add the chocolate. Make sure the chocolate is unsweetened. Baker's is the only one generally available. When the chocolate is melted, put aside to cool. Put the eggs, sugar, salt and vanilla into a mixer bowl and beat until light and fluffy. Then turn the mixer to low speed and add the flour, or fold in by hand. Add the chocolate and pecans and mix well, scraping down the sides of the bowl with a rubber spatula. Line a jelly-roll pan with parchment paper, oil the paper lightly and pour the batter into the pan. Bake about 25 minutes or until the top is dry. Remove brownies from oven, cool and put into the freezer in the pan before you try to cut them.

The reason these are fudge brownies is they are not fully baked. They are actually underbaked so that the center stays very moist. Because your oven may be too hot, you must check them after 20 minutes. If the top is dry, test the middle with a sharp knife. If the brownies are very liquid inside they are not done, but if the center has the consistency of chocolate pudding, they are. Baking generally will take 24 to 28 minutes.

To cut the brownies, make sure they are very cold throughout. Then cut them in the pan with a pizza cutter. Turn the pan over, peel off the parchment paper and separate. Keep frozen or refrigerated.

Yield: approximately 3 dozen brownies

Almond and Anise Bread

This used to be to me what fudge brownies are now; and since it is very easy to make, I thought you might like to have the recipe. It also makes a great bread for a brunch or a great Christmas gift. I suggest, though, that in that case you make it in small loaf pans, as otherwise, you have to start baking around December 1. And remember, once you get your friends used to gifts like that, they expect them every Christmas.

⅔ *cup finely chopped blanched almonds*

2½ *cups all purpose-flour*

2 *teaspoons baking powder*

½ *teaspoon salt*

½ *cup butter, softened*

1 *cup sugar*

1 *teaspoon anise seed*

¼ *teaspoon almond extract*

5 *eggs*

Spread the almonds evenly on a cookie sheet and toast in a 450° F. oven for 5 minutes. Stir occasionally. Set aside and cool.

Sift the flour, baking powder and salt, and set aside. Put the butter in a mixer bowl and beat until fluffy. Add the sugar, beat until well blended, then add the anise seed, almond extract and the eggs, one at a time. Beat until light and fluffy, then add the dry ingredients and almonds.

Turn the batter into a 9″ × 5″ × 3″ loaf pan that has been well greased and bake in a 350° F. oven for 60 to 65 minutes.

Yield: 1 loaf

Peach Muffins

I am writing this chapter in the month of August, and I am surrounded by one of God's greatest gifts: fresh fruit from New Jersey.

My love affair with New Jersey fruit and vegetables began some years ago when I was lucky enough to meet Philip Alampi, Secretary of Agriculture for that state. Phil is truly a remarkable person. He has held this position through many changes of administration, not because he is a politician, but because he is an efficient administrator and a very progressive thinker. A master of persuasion, he works tirelessly to improve farming in New Jersey. He believes, as I do, that good agriculture can work for the benefit of both the farmer and the consumer.

At any rate, through my friendship with Phil, I have met many of the state's leading producers of fruit and vegetables. Each year they have a meeting in Princeton of all the heads of the various councils: Blueberry Council, Peach Council, etc., and while the men have their business meeting, I give a cooking class for the wives. Afterwards, we all enjoy cocktails at the governor's mansion.

I don't charge a fee for this class. I only ask that each person bring a case of their most perfect freshly picked produce. Then I load up a panel truck and take it to New York, call all my friends and have a feast. One year, Joe and I ate two dozen ears of fresh white sweet corn at two in the morning.

The idea for this exchange came to me when I was studying American history to pass my citizenship exam. I read how the settlers used to barter with the Indians. I can tell you that those settlers never had it as good as this settler!

2	cups sifted all-purpose flour
½	teaspoon salt
1	tablespoon baking powder
¾	cup granulated sugar
1	egg
1	cup milk
4	tablespoons melted butter (½ stick)
1½–2	cups diced fresh peaches

Preheat oven to 425° F. Sift flour, salt, baking powder and sugar together into a bowl. Beat egg well in a Pyrex cup. Add milk and melted butter. Then add liquid to flour. Stir with a wooden spoon just enough to combine ingredients. Don't overmix!

Peel and dice fresh ripe peaches about the size of sugar cubes and fold into the batter. Pour batter into well-greased muffin tins, filling each cup about two-thirds full. Bake about 18 to 20 minutes, or until the muffins are nicely browned. If you can find the 5-ounce Pyrex cups used for popovers, they can also be used to make spectacular muffins.

Yield: approximately 2 dozen

Desserts

There is one surefire way to have a successful dinner party—serve three different great desserts. Being the last course, it is the one your guests will remember the most. You can get away with a mediocre first course, but never with a bad dessert. These days, the dessert course is no longer a part of the everyday meal, so you should put aside all thought of calories when you do serve desserts.

When you make desserts, follow these simple rules:

1. Use the best ingredients available. If you want to economize, don't have a dinner party.
2. Do not use artificial flavors or artificial toppings. The practice of making homemade desserts, then putting canned whipped chemicals on top is ridiculous.
3. When serving fruit, make sure it is the very best; if not, don't serve it.
4. Never use food coloring.

The dishes in this chapter range from light to sinfully rich. I leave the choice to you. If, as I do, you serve several desserts at one time, balance them by color, texture and richness.

Note: I use fruit brandies a great deal in my cooking, especially framboise, kirsch and calvados. Whenever you buy them, buy the best, which generally comes from Europe; framboise from Alsace, kirsch from the Black Forest and calvados from Normandy. After all, their whole purpose is to enhance the flavor.

Poached Peaches in Wine

A few years ago, my daughter and I went to visit Pat and Doug Zee at the Zee Orchards in Glassboro, New Jersey, one of the major peach farms in the state. Doug loaded us into his station wagon and said, "Let's go see your peach tree." We drove through his orchards for about 15 minutes until we came to a tree that was fenced off from the rest. Doug said, "I told my pickers to save this one for you." This tree was laden with the most spectacular ripe peaches you can imagine. They were the size of golden softballs, dragging the branches almost to the ground. We all sat under the tree and ate a few peaches and, I am embarrassed to say, let the peach juice run down our chins.

You don't have an experience like that very often, because peaches are a big business today. Very few are tree ripened, because they won't travel well. But you can find great peaches from all over this country. Look for ones that are still firm with yellowish color and a red blush. Never buy green peaches, they will shrivel instead of ripening.

6 peaches, peeled

Syrup:

   2 cups white wine

   2 cups water

1–1½ cups sugar, depending on the sweetness of the peaches

   1 whole vanilla bean

Raspberry Sauce:

   1 package frozen raspberries, thawed

   ½ cup red currant jelly

   1 tablespoon framboise (raspberry brandy), optional

   ½ tablespoon cornstarch

Put the wine, water, sugar and vanilla bean in a saucepan over medium heat. Bring to a boil, stirring occasionally, and simmer this syrup for 10 minutes. To peel your peaches, drop into boiling water for 20 seconds, then remove with a slotted spoon and peel off the skin with a paring knife. Then put them into the syrup and poach over gentle heat for about 10 to 20 minutes, covered. Test doneness by putting the point of a knife into the peach; there should be no resistance. The cooking time depends upon the size and ripeness of your peaches. Cool the peaches in the syrup, then remove from the syrup and arrange in a glass bowl. Pour the following raspberry sauce over them.

Put the raspberries, currant jelly, framboise and cornstarch into a blender and blend until well combined. Put this sauce through a strainer in order to remove the seeds. In a saucepan, bring the sauce to a gentle boil, stirring constantly in order to thicken. Turn off the heat, and cool before pouring over the arranged peaches.

Yield: 6 servings

Note: This syrup can be used to poach pears, apples, oranges or any other fruit you wish. You may replace the vanilla bean with 1 cinnamon stick, 3 cloves and the peel of 1 orange. The length of poaching time depends upon what type of fruit you use. If your peaches do not peel easily, they may not have been ripe enough. In that case, simply peel them with a vegetable peeler, which you also use for peeling pears.

Peaches Advocate

In 1825, that famous gastronome and wit, Brillat-Savarin, observed the following: "A well-fed man is not at all the same as a hungry one; that the table constitutes a kind of tie between the bargainer and the bargained-with and makes the diners more willing to receive certain impressions, to submit to certain influences; from this is born political gastronomy." This use of food power has not escaped me, either, and although I use brownies to open doors, I consider lunch at the Cookingschool my heavy artillery.

Among those I have for lunch are my lawyers, for although I don't need them often, when I do, I want them to give me their best. This recipe was created for them on their last visit.

6	*ripe peaches, peeled, cut in half, pits removed*
6	*teaspoons honey*
½	*cup cognac*
2	*tablespoons sesame seeds*
1	*cup heavy cream, whipped to very soft peaks with*
2	*tablespoons confectioners' sugar*

Place the peach halves in an ovenproof serving dish. Fill peach cavities with honey. Pour cognac over them and sprinkle the sesame seeds on top. Cover dish with aluminum foil and bake in a preheated 350° F. oven for 20 minutes. Serve warm with runny whipped cream on the side.

You can make the peaches ahead of time and put them in the oven when your guests arrive. For another variation, crumble an Amaretto cookie over each peach half in place of the honey and sesame seeds.

Yield: 6 servings

Fresh Fruit Kabobs

When I serve a selection of desserts, I generally try to include fresh fruits. I find the kabob method particularly effective because it is strikingly beautiful, and it does not require extra plates as in the case of fruit salad. I choose five of the most lush fruits I can find, keeping color and taste contrast in mind. Then I cut them into large bite-size pieces and fill a flat basket with ti leaves, or any other large decorative leaves, and lay the fruit skewers on the leaves in rows. Then I decorate the basket or platter with a few fresh flowers, such as gardenias or small white orchids.

Fresh strawberries, washed, dried and hulled

Kiwi fruit, peeled and cut into quarters

Fresh cantaloupe, peeled, seeded and cut into chunks

Fresh pineapple, peeled, cut into quarters, cored and cut into chunks

Fresh honeydew, peeled, seeded and cut into chunks

6-inch bamboo skewers

Skewer the fruits in the same order as they appear on the ingredients list. Wash ti leaves with cold water and dry; arrange in a circular or fan pattern. Arrange skewers on the leaves, side by side, and put a fresh flower in the middle.

Baked Bananas with Rum

6	*ripe bananas*
6	*tablespoons butter*
½	*cup brown sugar*
½	*cup dark rum*

Peel the bananas and cut them in half lengthwise. In a heavy sautéing pan, melt the butter, and when it starts to bubble, add the bananas and sauté them on both sides until lightly browned. Turn carefully with a spatula and fork, and do not overcook them. Transfer to a preheated serving platter.

Add the sugar and rum to the pan and heat until the sugar is dissolved. Pour over the bananas, or for extra showmanship, light the rum and pour it flaming over the bananas. This is particularly effective if you serve them from a chafing dish on a side table. This can be made ahead of time and gently reheated.

Yield: 6 servings

Oranges Flambé

The zest of 2 oranges

Juice of 2 oranges

2 tablespoons sugar

4 tablespoons butter or margarine

¼ cup Grand Marnier

6 oranges, peeled and segmented

¼ cup Grand Marnier for flambéing

Zest 2 oranges and squeeze, reserving juice and zest separately. Blanch zest in 2 cups of boiling water for 1 minute.

In a chafing dish, melt the sugar until it turns to caramel, then add the butter, ¼ cup Grand Marnier, orange juice and blanched zest. Simmer, stirring constantly, for about 2 minutes. Then add the orange segments, heat them but do not let liquid come to a boil. Heat ¼ cup Grand Marnier, set aflame and pour over the oranges.

Yield: 6 servings

Sorbets

I think the almost forgotten custom of serving a fruit sorbet between dinner courses is a wonderful tradition that should be revived. I do it quite often myself and it always adds elegance to a dinner party. The idea, of course, is to create a pause between the fish course and the main course and to refresh the palate.

The history of sorbet is a fascinating tale in itself. Marco Polo introduced sorbet, or flavored ice, to the Italian court in the late thirteenth century. He brought recipes for this wondrous dessert from the palace of the Kublai Khan, the emperor of China. This new discovery dazzled the Italians and then the French, but for many centuries to follow, only the nobility were to enjoy sorbets. Ships were sent north at great expense in those days to bring back blocks of ice, which were then stored in specially built underground cellars. Today sorbet is a little easier to make than it was in those "good old days," so here are some of my favorite recipes.

Pear Sorbet:

1	*cup water*
¾	*cup sugar*
1	*1-inch section of a vanilla bean*
4	*pears, peeled, cored and cut into cubes*
1	*tablespoon Williams' pear brandy, optional*

Combine the water, sugar and vanilla bean in a saucepan, bring to a boil, stirring constantly until the sugar is dissolved. Then add the pears, bring to a boil again, cover and simmer over low heat until the pears are soft. Test with the point of a knife since the cooking time is dependent upon ripeness of the pears. Cool the mixture and remove the vanilla bean. Pour mixture into a food processor or blender and, if you wish, add the brandy. Blend until smooth; then put into a Pyrex pie plate or bowl, cover with plastic wrap and put in your freezer. After sorbet is frozen, and just before serving time, return it to the food processor and mix until smooth, or simply put the ingredients into one of the great new ice-cream machines. Serve immediately in chilled glasses.

Yield: 3 cups

Note: You can keep the sorbet in serving glasses in the freezer for up to 30 minutes before serving; beyond that, it gets too hard. Some points to remember about sorbets: if you add too much sugar or too much fruit brandy or liqueur, the sorbet will not freeze hard enough; if you add too little sugar, it will freeze too hard.

Strawberry Sorbet:

1   *cup water*

¾   *cup sugar*

2   *pints fresh strawberries, washed, dried, hulled and cut in half*

Put the water and sugar in a saucepan and bring to a boil over low heat, stirring constantly until sugar is dissolved. Cool the syrup for about 5 minutes and pour over the strawberries in a bowl.

You don't want to cook the strawberries, because they will lose their color and get too mushy. Marinate them in the syrup for about 30 minutes and then proceed as in the pear sorbet. This method is always used for delicate fresh fruit such as raspberries, blueberries, blackberries, kiwi fruit, etc. The pear sorbet method should be used for such fruits as peaches, papaya, mango and pineapple.

Whenever you use fruit juice instead of whole fruit, follow the method in the next recipe, for Lime Sorbet, and simply reduce the amount of sugar for less acidic and sweeter fruit juices.

Yield: 3 cups

Lime Sorbet:

2   *cups water*

1   *cup sugar*

½   *cup fresh lime juice*
    Grated rind of 1 lime

Put the water and sugar in a saucepan and bring to a boil over low heat, stirring constantly until the sugar is dissolved. Remove from heat, add the lime juice and grated rind. Put the mixture into a shallow bowl to cool, cover with plastic wrap and freeze. Follow directions as in pear sorbet.

There are many beautiful ways to serve sorbets. You can serve this sorbet in scooped-out lime shells—the same with lemon—on a green leaf on a glass plate. At times, I have served poached peaches on beds of raspberry sorbet and poached pears on pear sorbet.

Yield: 3 cups

Frozen Raspberry Soufflé

There are few desserts as spectacular looking as a frozen soufflé. When we cater a large buffet, we make several flavors, and the brilliant colors really light up the dessert table. Do not make your frozen soufflés more than two days ahead of time because the gelatin tends to become rubbery.

This very same recipe can also be used to make strawberry soufflé. I use 4 eggs rather than 8 for both raspberry and strawberry. This is because it is necessary to use more fruit puree than other flavorings to achieve a full-bodied flavor and robust color.

4 eggs

¾ cup sugar

2 packages unflavored gelatin, dissolved in

¼ cup water (see page 18 for method)

2 packages frozen raspberries, partially thawed, put through a blender and strained to remove seeds

2 cups heavy cream, whipped to soft peaks

Beat the eggs and sugar in the bowl of an electric mixer for about 10 minutes until light and creamy. Add the dissolved gelatin slowly to the beaten eggs, then add the raspberry puree with the mixer on low speed. Fold in the whipped cream and pour into a prepared soufflé dish. Put in the freezer for 2 to 3 hours, remove the waxed-paper collar and decorate the soufflé with whipped cream put through a pastry bag, raspberries, and fresh mint leaves.

Yield: 12 servings

Note: To prepare a soufflé dish, firmly tie a waxed-paper collar around it so that the collar extends 2 or 3 inches above the rim of the dish.

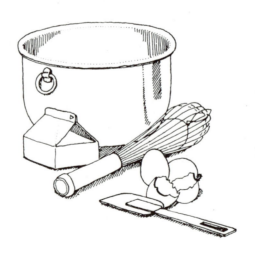

Frozen Mandarine Soufflé

8 eggs

½ cup sugar

2 packages unflavored gelatin, dissolved in

Juice of 1 orange

½ cup Mandarine Napoléon liqueur

1 tablespoon grated orange rind

2 cups heavy cream, whipped to soft peaks

Beat the eggs and sugar in a mixer bowl for about 10 minutes, until light and creamy. Add dissolved gelatin to the eggs, combining well, then add the liqueur slowly to the beaten eggs, along with the grated orange rind. Fold in the whipped cream and put soufflé in the freezer for at least 2 hours. At serving time, remove the paper collar and decorate the soufflé with the whipped cream put through a pastry bag, mandarin orange sections and fresh mint leaves.

Yield: 12 servings

Note: See instructions for preparing a soufflé dish in the recipe for Frozen Raspberry Soufflé, page 142. See page 18 for method of dissolving gelatin.

Here are some other flavoring suggestions ror soufflés:

Grand Marnier Soufflé.

Add ½ cup of Grand Marnier instead of the Mandarine Napoléon liqueur, and dissolve your gelatin in ¼ cup orange juice. All other ingredients and the method stay the same.

Praline Soufflé.

Add 1 cup praline paste—put through a food processor with a little milk if necessary to soften it—instead of the Mandarine Napoléon liqueur. Dissolve your gelatin in ¼ cup cognac and eliminate the orange rind. All other ingredients and the method stay the same.

Chestnut Soufflé.

Add 2 cups sweetened chestnut puree; soften if necessary the same way as the praline paste. Again eliminate the Mandarine Napoléon liqueur and orange rind. Dissolve the gelatin in ¼ cup rum.

Note: When decorating a soufflé, always coordinate the decoration with the flavor of the soufflé itself. For example, use praline powder (or candied violets if you don't want to make the praline powder) for the Praline Soufflé, or carameled chestnuts for the Chestnut Soufflé. Whatever you decorate with, stay away from maraschino cherries unless you make a maraschino soufflé.

Dessert Omelettes

Sweet omelettes are a spectacular dessert that you can whip up in no time. The following three are just some examples that you can make even more special; for instance, flambé the Grand Marnier omelette with some Grand Marnier, or how about folding some fresh raspberries into the vanilla one. Just go ahead and have fun with them. Once you know the basics, the rest is easy.

Lemon Soufflé Omelette.

Here is the recipe for a basic soufflé omelette with lemon juice added. The other recipes use different flavorings.

3	*eggs, separated*
3	*tablespoons granulated sugar*
3	*tablespoons lemon juice*
	Rind of ½ lemon, grated
	Confectioners' sugar
2	*lemon slices for decoration*

Combine the egg yolks, 2 tablespoons of the sugar, the lemon juice and rind and beat until fluffy. Then beat the egg whites with the rest of the sugar until stiff. Melt the butter in a heavy omelette pan. Fold the egg-yolk mixture gently into the egg whites and pour into the pan. Cook over low heat for about 3 minutes, making sure the mixture does not stick to the sides of the pan, then put the skillet under a broiler until the omelette puffs up and is golden brown. Slide the omelette onto a preheated serving platter. Dust with the confectioners' sugar and decorate with the lemon slices. Serve immediately.

Yield: 2 servings

Grand Marnier Omelette.

Add 3 tablespoons of Grand Marnier, cut the sugar to 2 tablespoons and leave out the lemon juice and rind. Otherwise, follow same directions as for lemon omelette.

Vanilla Omelette.

Add ½ tablespoon of pure vanilla extract or vanilla seeds from ¼ of a bean and leave out the lemon juice and rind. Serve omelette with some raspberry sauce over it. You will find the Raspberry Sauce recipe on page 136.

Crêpe a l'Orange

If you own a chafing dish, this is a spectacular dessert to serve. Since it can be made several days in advance, you can serve it without going into a frazzle.

Crêpes:

1	cup milk
3	eggs
1	cup all-purpose flour
1	tablespoon butter, melted
1	tablespoon cognac
1	tablespoon butter for cooking crêpes

Put all the ingredients for the crêpes into a blender and blend until smooth. Let this batter rest for 30 minutes. Make the crêpes in a 7-inch frying pan and let them cool, keeping them in the refrigerator until ready to fill.

Filling:

1	pint good vanilla ice cream, slightly softened
¼	cup Grand Marnier
	The zest of 1 orange

Combine all ingredients for the filling in a bowl and mix very thoroughly. Then cover with plastic wrap and put into the freezer until filling has hardened. Put about 3 tablespoons of this ice cream on the end of each crêpe and roll it up like a cigar. Put on a plate and keep in the freezer. When you have filled all your crêpes, cover plate with plastic wrap and keep in the freezer until ready to serve—at least 2 hours, or up to 3 days, ahead of time.

Sauce:

5	tablespoons butter
4	tablespoons sugar
½	cup fresh orange juice
½	cup Grand Marnier
2	oranges, skin removed, segmented
	The zest of 1 orange

At serving time, make your sauce by melting the butter in a skillet or chafing dish. Add the sugar and stir until dissolved, then add rest of ingredients and bring to a boil. Simmer this sauce gently for about 3 minutes. Put filled crêpes straight from the freezer onto a serving dish and pour the hot sauce over them. Serve immediately.

Yield: 6 to 8 crêpes

Crêpes Normandy

Every so often, I wake up in the middle of the night and think of a new recipe by wondering what would happen if I would . . . Well, this recipe is the result of one such awakening and has turned into a most popular dish. The name stems from the fact that the Normandy region of France is well known for its calvados and rich crème fraîche. You can make the crêpes as well as the sauce ahead of time, and then reheat the sauce and fill the crêpes with it.

Crêpes:

3   *eggs*

1   *cup milk*

1   *cup all-purpose flour*

1   *tablespoon calvados (French apple brandy)*

2   *tablespoons butter, melted*

1   *tablespoon butter for cooking crêpes*

To make the crêpe batter, put the eggs, milk, flour, calvados and melted butter in your blender and blend until smooth. Let this batter rest for 30 minutes. Make crêpes in a 7-inch frying pan, then fold into quarters and keep warm.

Sauce:

½   *cup sugar*

4   *tablespoons butter*

2   *apples, peeled, cored and sliced*

½   *cup apple juice*

¼   *cup calvados*

   Crème fraîche (see below)

To make the sauce, melt the sugar until caramelized, then add the butter and apples, combining well, then add apple juice and simmer gently for a few minutes. Heat the calvados, pour the apple mixture over the crêpes, light the calvados and pour over the crêpes. Serve the crème fraîche on the side.

Crème Fraîche:

1   *cup heavy cream (not ultrapasteurized)*

2   *tablespoons buttermilk*

Combine cream with buttermilk, mixing well. Cover lightly with plastic wrap (do not seal) and leave at room temperature for about 24 hours, at which point it will have thickened. Then keep refrigerated until serving time. It will last for at least 5 days in your refrigerator.

Yield: 6 to 8 crêpes

Note: The crème fraîche recipe will only work with fresh heavy cream. If it is not available, simply whip some heavy cream to light peaks, or mix 1 cup sour cream with ½ cup of heavy cream, and serve on the side.

Oeufs à la Neige

There is no doubt that this is the most spectacular of all custard desserts. It is similar to Floating Island—about the same way a Mercedes-Benz is similar to a Volkswagen. Here the presentation is everything.

To avoid big problems whenever you cook custards and custard sauces, you must be aware of why things are happening. Custards are thickened when the egg yolks get hot enough, and custards will curdle when the egg yolks come to a boil. That's the fine line you have to walk when you make a custard or hollandaise sauce. I always keep a bowl filled with ice water next to the stove when I make a custard sauce. If I see the sauce is about to boil, I plunge the saucepan into the ice water to stop the cooking. By taking this precaution, you can make your custards in a saucepan—provided, of course, that you have a good saucepan—rather than in a double boiler, which takes twice as long.

I find it much easier to shape the meringues with an ice-cream scoop than with 2 spoons. I bought one extra-large scoop especially for this purpose since I like my meringues to look like huge snowballs. Have a bowl of hot water next to you to rinse off the scoop after you make each meringue. I find that the traditional way of poaching meringues in milk makes them slightly soggy, so I prefer poaching them in water. Line a jelly-roll pan with two layers of paper towels to put the meringues on after poaching. You can make the custard itself the day before and the meringues in the morning, leaving them on the jelly-roll pan until ready to use; they do not need refrigeration. At serving time, pile the meringues on top of the custard in a pyramid and drizzle the caramel on top. This step should not be done too far ahead of time, as the caramel melts and does not look as pretty. Why not make a show of it and do it in front of your guests as I do? If you are worried, practice the first time with your family.

Custard:

3	cups milk
1	cup heavy cream
8	egg yolks
1¾	cups sugar
1	teaspoon pure vanilla extract

Heat the milk and cream in a saucepan; make sure not to let come to a boil. In the meantime, put the egg yolks, sugar and vanilla into a mixing bowl and beat until light and fluffy. Add the hot milk and cream to the egg yolks very slowly, mixing at a low speed, then pour the mixture either into a double boiler or heavy saucepan and cook it, stirring constantly until it starts to thicken and coats the back of a metal spoon. Stand the pan in ice water in order to stop all cooking. Cool the custard and pour into your serving dish. Cover with plastic wrap and put in the refrigerator to chill.

Meringues:

8	egg whites
1½	cups superfine sugar

Beat the egg whites in your mixer until they start to form peaks, then slowly add your superfine sugar and continue mixing until the egg whites form stiff peaks. Pour 2 inches of water into a large sautéing pan and heat, but do not let boil. Then take an ice-cream scoop, or 2 spoons, and form the egg whites into balls; poach them gently in the sautéing pan for about 2 minutes on each side, then lift them with a slotted spoon onto a paper-lined tray. At serving time put meringues on your custard and drizzle some caramel over them.

Caramel:

1 cup sugar	Put the sugar in a heavy sautéing pan and melt it over medium heat, stirring occasionally, until it turns caramel colored. Let the caramel cool for a few minutes until it starts to thicken, then take a fork and drizzle it in a back-and-forth motion over your meringues.

Yield: 8 servings

Note: If you let the water boil while poaching the meringues, they will disintegrate. If you have difficulty turning the meringues while poaching, just leave them to poach a few extra minutes without turning.

Whenever you work with caramel be very careful, as it is extremely hot. While making it, do not walk away; watch it carefully, as it can burn easily.

Vanilla Bavarian Cream

Now that you have learned all about cooking custards in the recipe for Oeufs à la Neige, you might as well try Bavarian cream, which starts out as a custard sauce and, by the addition of gelatin and whipped cream, ends up a heavenly creation. I generally put it into a ring mold, and after unmolding it, fill the center with fresh strawberries or raspberries. It looks spectacular, and everyone loves it.

Instead of vanilla, you could flavor the cream with ½ cup Grand Marnier, or melt 3 ounces of bittersweet chocolate and add that and ¼ cup strong coffee to make a mocha-flavored Bavarian cream.

2 cups milk	In a heavy saucepan, scald the milk, that is, heat it over low heat until just before the boiling point. Beat egg yolks, vanilla and sugar until creamy. Pour the heated milk gradually into the egg mixture, stirring constantly. Cook mixture in a double boiler over simmering water, stirring constantly until it coats the back of the spoon. Remove from heat and add softened gelatin. Stir until dissolved. Pour custard into a bowl and cool in the refrigerator until it starts to thicken, or stand the bowl in another bowl filled with ice cubes and cold water. This will speed up the process. Stir custard occasionally with a
6 egg yolks	
Seed of ½ vanilla bean or 1 teaspoon pure vanilla extract	
¾ cup sugar	
1½ packages gelatin softened in	

¼ cup cold water

1 cup heavy cream,
  whipped

whisk to cool evenly. Then fold in the whipped cream. Pour into a mold and refrigerate overnight.

To unmold, dip the mold in hot water for a few seconds, cover with serving platter and invert. Decorate with whipped cream, sliced strawberries, and mint leaves.

Yield: 8 servings

Note: When cooling the custard, make sure to check it. You don't want it to thicken too much, otherwise you cannot fold in the whipped cream properly and will end up with lumps. The thickness of the custard should be that of egg whites.

Bavarian Royal

This is the ultimate way to serve Bavarian cream and is really not that difficult to master. Basically, you first make a jelly roll, then you slice the jelly roll into thin rounds and place them into a bowl to cover the entire inside surface. Then fill the bowl with Bavarian cream and allow to set. At serving time, invert the bowl and unmold a spectacular dome. Be the first on your block to make it.

5 egg yolks

¼ cup sugar

5 egg whites

¼ cup sugar

¼ cup all-purpose flour
  and

¼ cup cornstarch, sifted
  together

1 recipe Vanilla
  Bavarian Cream (see
  page 148)

In a mixer, beat the egg yolks and ¼ cup sugar until light and fluffy. In a separate bowl, beat the egg whites until foamy, then add ¼ cup sugar slowly and continue mixing until they form stiff peaks. (Do not overmix.) Fold the egg whites into the egg yolks carefully but thoroughly, and then fold in the flour and cornstarch mixture.

Put into a 13" × 18" × 1" jelly-roll pan that you have lined with parchment paper and bake in preheated 400° F. oven for 15 to 20 minutes.

When you have finished baking the cake, cool it for awhile, then unmold onto a towel, trim the edges and spread with raspberry jam. Roll it up, let rest for awhile, then cut into thin slices. Line the inside of a round stainless-steel bowl with them, making sure they touch each other as closely as possible. Then pour the Vanilla Bavarian Cream into this lined bowl, cover with plastic wrap and refrigerate overnight. To unmold, dip the bowl into hot water for a few seconds and invert onto your serving platter. Decorate with whipped cream.

Yield: 10 servings

Coeur de Crème Tart

Coeur de crème always has been one of my most popular desserts, and in this recipe we have taken it one step further. It looks terrific, is easy to make and tastes fabulous. It's one of those recipes that establishes you as a good cook. You can make the tart itself a day, or for that matter, several days ahead of time. You can also make individual tarts instead of the 10-inch round tart in this recipe. The coeur de crème itself has to be made the day before. I suggest that you do the final assembling not more than a few hours before serving since this will keep your crust crisper.

1   *Hazelnut Crust (see page 123)*

½   *pound cream cheese (Philadelphia brand), at room temperature*

½   *cup confectioners' sugar*

     The seeds of 1 vanilla bean

2   *cups heavy cream*

1   *pint fresh strawberries, washed, dried and hulled*

½   *jar currant jelly, melted and cooled until it starts to thicken*

     Fresh mint leaves for decoration

Make the Hazelnut Crust and follow the procedures for baking it blind (see page 120). Cool the crust.

Put the cream cheese into the bowl of an electric mixer and beat until light and fluffy. Then add the confectioners' sugar and vanilla seeds and continue mixing until well combined. If you have a good mixer, simply add the heavy cream to the cream-cheese mixture and continue beating until it is light and fluffy and forms soft peaks. Otherwise, whip the heavy cream separately until it forms soft peaks, and fold into the cream-cheese mixture by hand with a rubber spatula.

Wring out a clean Handi Wipe or cheesecloth in cold water and line a strainer or small colander with it. Put the coeur de crème mixture into it and stand in a bowl or pie dish. Cover with plastic wrap and refrigerate overnight. The next day, discard the milky liquid, called "whey," that has dripped into your bottom bowl or dish. Put the coeur de crème mixture into your baked and cooled tart shell. Cut the strawberries in half lengthwise and arrange them in concentric circles on top of the cream. Brush the strawberries with the melted and cooled currant jelly. Put a mint leaf in the middle and refrigerate for 30 minutes before serving.

Yield: 1 10-inch tart

Rum Raisin Rice Pudding

This is a recipe that my former partner, Joe, created, and it is still the greatest rice pudding I ever tasted.

1	cup white seedless raisins
1	cup Myers's Original Dark Rum
½	cup Carolina rice
2	cups water
	Salt
1	quart milk
½	cup sugar
4	egg yolks
2	cups milk
1	tablespoon vanilla extract
1½	cups heavy cream, whipped with
¼	cup confectioners' sugar

Soak the raisins in the dark rum a few hours, preferably overnight. Put the rice, water and a little salt into a saucepan, bring to a boil and cook for 5 minutes. Drain, rinse with cold water and return to saucepan. Add the quart of milk and ½ cup sugar and bring to boil. Lower heat and simmer for about 45 minutes, uncovered, until most of the milk is absorbed.

In a bowl, beat the egg yolks lightly. Add the 2 cups milk, the vanilla extract, the raisins and about 2 tablespoons of the rum, and mix. Pour this into the rice and continue stirring until the mixture has thickened, but do not let it boil. Remove from heat and refrigerate. When the pudding is thoroughly chilled, fold in the sweetened whipped cream and serve.

Yield: 8 servings

Chocolate Mousse Albert

I don't believe there is such a thing as too many chocolate mousse recipes, so here is a simple one that I named for Albert Kumin, who has taught me more about desserts than I thought possible. My famous more elaborate recipe follows.

6 ounces bittersweet chocolate (Tobler)

3 tablespoons kahlua

3 tablespoons orange juice

½ cup roasted and ground filberts

2 egg yolks

2 whole eggs

1 teaspoon vanilla extract

½ cup sugar

1 cup heavy cream, lightly whipped

Over low heat melt the chocolate in the kahlua and orange juice and add the ground filberts. Set aside to cool. Put the egg yolks, whole eggs, vanilla and sugar in the bowl of an electric mixer and beat until light and fluffy. Add the melted and cooled chocolate and filberts, fold together until smooth, then add the whipped cream, folding it in by hand. Pour into a bowl or individual cups and freeze for several hours.

Yield: 4 to 6 servings

Chocolate Mousse Normandy

Since this one particular dessert changed the course of my career, and since it is one of the most delectable of all creations, I must start this recipe with its story.

In 1965, I had gone to an employment agency looking for a job as a chef. I was twenty-one and had no credentials or experience as a chef in America, but I had a fierce determination to bluff it through. At the time, Billy Rose had commissioned this agency to find him a new chef. When I saw the notice on the bulletin board, I knew he was somebody important, but I wasn't sure why. I applied for the job and surprisingly was given an appointment for an interview. In the meantime, I asked everyone about Billy Rose. Somebody mentioned his book Wine, Women and Words. *I went to the public library and read every word carefully over and over until I felt I knew all about him.*

The day of the interview I was intoxicated by my own self-confidence. I was going to conquer the great Billy Rose. I was brought into his presence by the butler and was a little surprised by his small size; from his story, I had imagined him six feet tall. "You're a chef?" he asked incredulously. I was a little shaken, but I replied quite coolly, "You can't judge a book by its cover, Mr. Rose." He liked that, I guess, because he didn't have me thrown out. He asked me several questions about cookery, some about salary (being a millionaire didn't make him overly generous) and finally asked, "Can you make Chocolate Mousse Normandy?" "Of course," I replied. "What's your recipe?" he asked. "Mr. Rose," I rejoined, "I make it a policy to give my recipes to no one." Whereupon he hired me and told me to report in three days.

It was not until I had walked in a daze for some blocks that I realized I had never heard of Chocolate Mousse Normandy. I rushed home to my sizable collection of cookbooks to find it. Not there. Frantically, I called friends, chefs, magazines. I couldn't sleep. I thought maybe Billy Rose was playing a cruel joke on me. Finally, on the third day, in desperation I went to the New York Public Library on 42nd Street. I leafed through every cookbook on their shelves. And then, I found it—in one of Dionne Lucas's books. (I discovered later that she had once worked for Mr. Rose.) It was a moment of tremendous relief. I made it for him the first night, and have been making it ever since, with a few variations of my own. Chocolate Mousse Normandy is truly one of the great chocolate desserts and has, since the years with Billy, gotten me all sorts of great things. You can make it a week ahead, if you wish, and keep it in the freezer until 15 minutes before serving time.

If you are unable to get chocolate Cat Tongues (they are made by Feodora and look like ladyfingers), you can simply line the sides of the springform pan with waxed paper and remove it at serving time.

2	packages chocolate Cat Tongues (Feodora)
2	tablespoons butter (to stick Cat Tongues to mold)
¾	pound bittersweet chocolate
10	tablespoons light rum
1½	sticks (6 ounces) butter, at room temperature
½	cup confectioners' sugar
4	egg yolks
½	cup salted almonds, finely ground
2½	cups heavy cream
¼	cup confectioners' sugar

Cut a circle of waxed paper exactly to fit the bottom of an 8-inch springform pan. Line the sides of this mold with the Cat Tongues, putting a speck of butter on their flat sides and then sticking them to the inside walls of the mold, standing upright. Be most careful not to leave gaps or spaces between them. Make the mousse as follows and fill the lined mold with it.

Break the chocolate into small pieces and melt it in a small, heavy pan together with the rum over a low heat, stirring constantly. When the chocolate is melted, take it off the heat and cool, but do not let it set.

In the bowl of an electric mixer, cream the 1½ sticks butter until light and fluffy, then add the ½ cup confectioners' sugar and beat well. Add the egg yolks, one at a time, the almonds and—finally—the cooled chocolate.

In another bowl, whip the heavy cream until it begins to thicken, then add the ¼ cup sugar and the vanilla bean seeds. Continue beating until the cream is stiff enough to hold its shape.

Put one-quarter of the cream aside for decorating and fold the rest, together with the beaten egg whites, into the chocolate mixture. Pour into the prepared mold. Cover with plastic wrap and freeze for 2 hours.

To remove the mousse from the mold, run a knife carefully between mold and Cat Tongues and invert onto

½   vanilla bean, seeds
only

4   egg whites, beaten to
soft peaks

Satin ribbon,
candied violets, for
decoration

a flat serving dish. Remove the circle of waxed paper from the top and decorate mousse as follows:

Fit a pastry bag with a rosette tube and fill with the reserved whipped cream. Pipe rosettes of cream around the edge of the top of the mousse and place a candied violet on each one. Tie the ribbon around the sides (to cover the spots of butter on the Cat Tongues) and, if you like, put a fresh flower in the bow.

Yield: 10 to 12 servings

Index